Theories and Things

Theories and Things

W. V. Quine

The Belknap Press of
Harvard University Press
Cambridge, Massachusetts
and London, England

Copyright © 1981 by the President and Fellows of Harvard College
All rights reserved
Printed in the United States of America

10 9 8 7 6 5 4

Library of Congress Cataloging in Publication Data

Quine, W. V. (Willard Van Orman)
  Theories and things.

  Bibliography: p.
  Includes index.
  1. Philosophy—Miscellanea.   I. Title.
B68.Q56   191   81–4517
ISBN 0–674–87925–2 (cloth)   AACR2
ISBN 0–674–87926–0 (paper)

To

Bob and Rosalie

Preface

The first and longest essay in this collection, very nearly a title essay, is a decoction of several of my recent papers and lectures on what the assuming of objects means and how it helps. Four subsequent essays are new to the literature; two of these may still reappear in colloquium proceedings. The remaining twenty-one items in the collection are garnered from scattered publications and revised none or in varying degrees. Seven of them date from the sixties; the rest are recent, two being still in press as I write.

Themes of ontology, epistemology, and semantics are pursued in the first five essays. Then comes an unaccustomed venture into ethics, followed by three pieces on philosophy in retrospect and two reviews of contemporary philosophers of science. Essays 12 to 14, next, reflect my dim view of intensional objects and modal logic. The ensuing six are occupied with logic proper, or what I deem proper, and the nature of mathematics. The next item, number 21, is less essay than medley, and it is followed by a short piece on metaphor and two on public relations. The drift away from philosophy becomes complete in two essays with which the book concludes. They are two examples from among six reviews in geography and lexicography that I wrote in a somewhat playful spirit in the sixties, and I include them in that same spirit. They do not add to the philosophical content which it is the purpose of this volume to convey.

In many of these essays, as in previous writings, I have been helped by suggestions from Burton Dreben. To him and to David Kaplan and Donald Davidson I am indebted also for good advice regarding the volume as a whole.

Harvard University
February 1981

Contents

Theories and Things

1

❧ Things and Their Place in Theories

Our talk of external things, our very notion of things, is just a conceptual apparatus that helps us to foresee and control the triggering of our sensory receptors in the light of previous triggering of our sensory receptors. The triggering, first and last, is all we have to go on.

In saying this I too am talking of external things, namely,

This is a revised and amplified version of "What is it all about?" an essay first published by the United Chapters of Phi Beta Kappa in *The American Scholar*, Winter 1980–1981. That essay was the Gail Caldwell Stine Memorial Lecture that I gave at Mount Holyoke College in April 1980 and soon afterward at Oakland University in Michigan, Uppsala University in Sweden, and the University of Iceland. The content derived largely from two of my four Immanuel Kant Lectures (Stanford University, February 1980) and developed out of lectures that I gave ten to twelve months earlier at Tallahassee, Ann Arbor, Berkeley, Los Angeles, Madison, Louvain-la-Neuve, Aix-en-Provence, and the Collège de France under such titles as "How and why to reify" and "Les étapes de la réification."

The present version incorporates substantial passages also from three other publications: "Whither physical objects?" (*Boston Studies in the Philosophy of Science*, vol. 39, pp. 497–504, copyright © 1976, D. Reidel Publishing Co., Dordrecht, Holland), "Facts of the matter" (R. Shahan, ed., *American Philosophy from Edwards to Quine*, Norman: University of Oklahoma Press, 1977), and "The variable and its place in reference" (Z. van Straaten, ed., *Philosophical Subjects: Essays Presented to P. F. Strawson*, Oxford: Oxford University Press, 1980). Bits are drawn also from my replies to critics in three periodicals now in press: *Sintaxis* (Montevideo), the *Southwestern Journal of Philosophy*, and *Midwest Studies in Philosophy*.

people and their nerve endings. Thus what I am saying applies in particular to what I am saying, and is not meant as skeptical. There is nothing we can be more confident of than external things—some of them, anyway—other people, sticks, stones. But there remains the fact—a fact of science itself—that science is a conceptual bridge of our own making, linking sensory stimulation to sensory stimulation; there is no extrasensory perception.

I should like now to consider how this bridging operation works. What does it mean to assume external objects? And what about objects of an abstract sort, such as numbers? How do objects of both sorts help us in developing systematic connections between our sensory stimulations?

The assuming of objects is a mental act, and mental acts are notoriously difficult to pin down—this one more than most. Little can be done in the way of tracking thought processes except when we can put words to them. For something objective that we can get our teeth into we must go after the words. Words accompany thought for the most part anyway, and it is only as thoughts are expressed in words that we can specify them.

If we turn our attention to the words, then what had been a question of assuming objects becomes a question of verbal *reference* to objects. To ask what the *assuming* of an object consists in is to ask what *referring* to the object consists in.

We refer by using words, and these we learn through more or less devious association with stimulations of our sensory receptors. The association is direct in cases where the word is learned by ostension. It is thus that the child learns to volunteer the word 'milk', or to assent if the word is queried, in the conspicuous presence of milk; also to volunteer the word so as to induce the presence of milk.

The mechanism in such a case is relatively clear and simple, as psychological mechanisms go. It is the conditioning of a response. To call it objective reference, however, is premature. Learning the expression 'milk' in this way, by direct association with appropriate stimulations, is the same in principle as learning the sentence 'It's windy' or 'It's cold' or 'It's raining' by direct association with appropriate stimulations. It is we in our adult ontological sophistication that recognize the word 'milk' as referring to an object, a substance, while we are less ready to single out an object of reference for 'It's windy' or 'It's cold' or 'It's raining'. This is the contrast that we need eventually to analyze if we are to achieve a satisfactory analysis of what to count as objective reference; and it is not a contrast that obtrudes in the primitive phase of learning by ostension. The word 'milk', when uttered in recognition or when queried and assented to, is best regarded at first as a sentence on a par with 'It's windy', 'It's cold', and the rest; it is as if to say 'It's milk'. It is a one-word sentence. All of these examples are *occasion* sentences, true on some occasions of utterance and false on others. We are conditioned to assent to them under appropriate stimulation. There is no call to read into them, as yet, any reference to objects.

The view of sentences as primary in semantics, and of names or other words as dependent on sentences for their meaning, is a fruitful idea that began perhaps with Jeremy Bentham's theory of fictions.[1] What Bentham observed was that you have explained any term quite adequately if you have shown how all contexts in which you propose to use it can be paraphrased into antecedently intelligible language. When this is recognized, the philosophical analysis of concepts or explication of terms comes into its own. Sentences come to be seen as the primary repository of meaning, and words are seen as imbibing their meaning through their use in sentences.

Recognition of sentences as primary has not only expedited philosophical analysis; it has also given us a better picture of how language is actually learned. First we learn short sentences, next we get a line on various words through their use in those sentences, and then on that basis we manage to grasp longer sentences in which those same words recur. Accordingly the development leading from sensory stimulation to objective reference is to be seen as beginning with the flat conditioning of simple occasion sentences to stimulatory events, and advancing through stages more forthrightly identifiable with objective reference. We have

1. See Essay 7 below.

still to consider what the distinguishing traits of these further stages might be.

As long as the word 'milk' can be accounted for simply as an occasion sentence on a par with 'It's raining', surely nothing is added by saying that it is a name of something. Nothing really is said. Similarly for 'sugar', 'water', 'wood'. Similarly even for 'Fido' and 'Mama'. We would be idly declaring there to be designata of the words, counterparts, shadows, one apiece: danglers, serving only as honorary designata of expressions whose use as occasion sentences would continue as before.

The outlook changes when individuative words emerge: words like 'chair' and 'dog'. These differ from the previous examples in the complexity of what has to be mastered in learning them. By way of mastery of any of those previous words, all that was called for was the ability to pass a true-false test regarding points or neighborhoods taken one at a time. It is merely a question, in the case of Fido or milk, of what visible points are on Fido or on milk and what ones are not. To master 'dog' or 'chair', on the other hand, it is not enough to be able to judge of each visible point whether it is on a dog or chair; we have also to learn where one dog or chair leaves off and another sets in.

In the case of such words, individuative ones, the idea of objective reference seems less trivial and more substantial. The word 'dog' is taken to denote each of many things, each dog, and the word 'chair', each chair. It is no longer an idle one-to-one duplication, a mirroring of each word in an object dreamed up for that exclusive purpose. The chairs and dogs are indefinite in number and individually, for the most part, nameless. The 'Fido'-Fido principle, as Ryle called it, has been transcended.

However, this contrast between the individuatives and the previous words does not become detectable until a further device has become available: predication. The contrast emerges only when we are in a position to compare the predication 'Fido is a dog' with the predication 'Milk is white'. Milk's being white comes down to the simple fact that whenever you point at milk you point at white. Fido's being a dog does not come down to the simple fact that whenever you point at Fido you point at a dog: it involves that and more. For whenever you point at Fido's head you point at a dog, and yet Fido's head does not qualify as a dog.

It is in this rather subtle way that predication creates a difference between individuative terms and others. Prior to predication, such words as 'dog' and 'chair' differ in no pertinent way from 'milk' and 'Fido'; they are simple occasion sentences that herald, indifferently, the presence of milk, Fido, dog, chair.

Thus reference may be felt to have emerged when we take to predicating individuative terms, as in 'Fido is a dog'. 'Dog' then comes to qualify as a general term denoting each dog, and thereupon, thanks again to the predication 'Fido is a dog', the word 'Fido' comes at last to qualify as a singular term naming one dog. In view then of the analogy of 'Milk is white' to 'Fido is a dog', it becomes natural to view the word 'milk' likewise as a singular term naming something, this time not a body but a substance.

In *Word and Object* and *The Roots of Reference* I have speculated on how we learn individuative terms, predication, and various further essentials of our language. I will not go further into that, but will merely remind you of what some of these further essentials are. Along with singular predication, as in 'Milk is white' and 'Fido is a dog', we want plural predication: 'Dogs are animals'. Along with monadic general terms, moreover, such as 'dog' and 'animal', we want dyadic ones, such as 'part of', 'darker than', 'bigger than', and 'beside'; also perhaps triadic and higher. Also we want predication of these polyadic terms, at least in the singular: thus 'Mama is bigger than Fido', 'Fido is darker than milk'. Also we want the truth functions—'not', 'and', 'or'—by means of which to build compound sentences.

Now a further leap forward, as momentous as predication, is the *relative clause*. It is a way of segregating what a sentence says about an object, and packaging it as a complex general term. What the sentence

Mont Blanc is higher than the Matterhorn but the Matterhorn is steeper

says about the Matterhorn is packaged in the relative clause:

object that is not as high as Mont Blanc but is steeper.

Predicating this of the Matterhorn carries us back in effect
to the original sentence.

The grammar of relative clauses can be simplified by re-
writing them in the 'such that' idiom:

> object x such that Mont Blanc is higher than x but x is
> steeper.

This keeps the word order of the original sentence. The 'x'
is just a relative pronoun written in mathematical style. We
can change the letter to avoid ambiguity in case one relative clause is embedded in another.

The relative clause serves no purpose in singular predication, since such predication just carries us back to a sentence
of the original form. Where it pays off is in plural predication. Without relative clauses, the use of plural predication
is cramped by shortage of general terms. We could still say
'Dogs are animals' and perhaps 'Small dogs are amusing
animals', but it is only with the advent of relative clauses
that we can aspire to such heights as 'Whatever is salvaged
from the wreck belongs to the state'. It becomes:

> Objects x such that x is salvaged from the wreck are
> objects x such that x belongs to the state.

In general, where 'Fx' and 'Gx' stand for any sentences that
we are in a position to formulate about x, relative clauses
open the way to the plural predication:

> Objects x such that Fx are objects x such that Gx.

Once we have this equipment, we have the full benefit of
universal and existential quantification. This is evident if we
reflect that '$(x)Fx$' is equivalent to '(x) (if not Fx then
$Fx)$' and hence to:

> Objects x such that not Fx are objects x such that Fx.

I said that reference may be felt to emerge with the predicating of individuatives. However, it is better seen as emerg-
ing by degrees. Already at the start the sentences 'Fido'
and 'Milk', unlike 'It's raining', are learned by association
with distinctively salient portions of the scene. Typically the
salience is induced by pointing. Here already, in the selec-

tivity of salience, is perhaps a first step toward the eventual namehood of 'Fido' and 'Milk'. Predications such as 'Milk is white' further enhance this air of objective reference, hinging as they do on a coinciding of saliences. Thus contrast the predication 'Milk is white' with 'When night falls the lamps are lit'. 'When' here is a connective comparable to the truth functions; it just happens to deliver standing sentences rather than occasion sentences when applied to occasion sentences. 'Milk is white' likewise can be viewed as a standing sentence compounded of the occasion sentences 'Milk' and 'White', but it says more than 'When there is milk there is white'; it says '*Where* there is milk there is white'. The concentration on a special part of the scene is thus doubly emphasized, and in this I sense further rumblings of objective reference.

Predications such as 'Milk is white' still afford, even so, little reason for imputing objective reference. As already remarked, we might as well continue to use the purported names as occasion sentences and let the objects go. A finite and listed ontology is no ontology.

Predication of individuatives, next, as in 'Fido is a dog', heightens reference in two ways. The concentration on a special part of the scene is emphasized here more strongly still than in 'Milk is white', since Fido is required not merely to be contained in the scattered part of the world that is made up of dog; he is required to fill one of its discrete blobs. And the more telling point, already noted, is that 'dog' transcends the 'Fido'-Fido principle; dogs are largely nameless.

Even at this stage, however, the referential apparatus and its ontology are vague. Individuation goes dim over any appreciable time interval. Thus consider the term 'dog'. We would recognize any particular dog in his recurrences if we noticed some distinctive trait in him; a dumb animal would do the same. We recognize Fido in his recurrences in learning the occasion sentence 'Fido', just as we recognize further milk and sugar in learning 'Milk' and 'Sugar'. Even in the absence of distinctive traits we will correctly concatenate momentary canine manifestations as stages of the same **dog** as long as we keep watching. After any considerable lapse of observation, however, the question of identity of unspeci-

fied dogs simply does not arise—not at the rudimentary stage
of language learning. It scarcely makes sense until we are
in a position to say such things as that in general if *any* dog
undergoes such and such then in due course that *same* dog
will behave thus and so. This sort of general talk about long-
term causation becomes possible only with the advent of
quantification or its equivalent, the relative clause in plural
predication. Such is the dependence of individuation, in the
time dimension, upon relative clauses; and it is only with full
individuation that reference comes fully into its own.

With the relative clause at hand, objective reference is indeed full blown. In the relative clause the channel of reference is the relative pronoun 'that' or 'which', together with
its recurrences in the guise of 'it', 'he', 'her', and so on. Regi-
mented in symbolic logic, these pronouns give way to bound
variables of quantification. The variables range, as we say,
over all objects; they admit all objects as values. To assume
objects of some sort is to reckon objects of that sort among
the values of our variables.

II

What objects, then, do we find ourselves assuming? Certainly bodies. The emergence of reference endowed the occasion sentences 'Dog' and 'Animal' with the status of general terms denoting bodies, and the occasion sentences 'Fido'
and 'Mama' with the status of singular terms designating
bodies.

We can see how natural it is that some of the occasion
sentences ostensively learned should have been such as to
foreshadow bodies, if we reflect on the social character of
ostension. The child learns the occasion sentence from the
mother while they view the scene from their respective
vantage points, receiving somewhat unlike presentations.
The mother in her childhood learned the sentence in similarly
divergent circumstances. The sentence is thus bound to be
versatile, applying regardless of angle. Thus it is that the
aspects of a body in all their visual diversity are naturally
gathered under a single occasion sentence, ultimately a single
designation.

We saw how the reification of milk, wood, and other sub-stances would follow naturally and closely on that of bodies. Bodies are our paradigmatic objects, but analogy proceeds apace; nor does it stop with substances. Grammatical anal-ogy between general terms and singular terms encourages us to treat a general term as if it designated a single object, and thus we are apt to posit a realm of objects for the general terms to designate: a realm of properties, or sets. What with the nominalizing also of verbs and clauses, a vaguely varied and very untidy ontology grows up.

The common man's ontology is vague and untidy in two ways. It takes in many purported objects that are vaguely or inadequately defined. But also, what is more significant, it is vague in its scope; we cannot even tell in general which of these vague things to ascribe to a man's ontology at all, which things to count him as assuming. Should we regard grammar as decisive? Does every noun demand some array of denotata? Surely not; the nominalizing of verbs is often a mere stylistic variation. But where can we draw the line?

It is a wrong question; there is no line to draw. Bodies are assumed, yes; they are the things, first and foremost. Beyond them there is a succession of dwindling analogies. Various expressions come to be used in ways more or less parallel to the use of the terms for bodies, and it is felt that correspond-ing objects are more or less posited, *pari passu;* but there is no purpose in trying to mark an ontological limit to the dwindling parallelism.

My point is not that ordinary language is slipshod, slip-shod though it be. We must recognize this grading off for what it is, and recognize that a fenced ontology is just not implicit in ordinary language. The idea of a boundary be-tween being and nonbeing is a philosophical idea, an idea of technical science in a broad sense. Scientists and philoso-phers seek a comprehensive system of the world, and one that is oriented to reference even more squarely and utterly than ordinary language. Ontological concern is not a correc-tion of a lay thought and practice; it is foreign to the lay cul-ture, though an outgrowth of it.

We can draw explicit ontological lines when desired. We can regiment our notation, admitting only general and singu-

lar terms, singular and plural predication, truth functions,
and the machinery of relative clauses; or, equivalently and
more artificially, instead of plural predication and relative
clauses we can admit quantification. Then it is that we can
say that the objects assumed are the values of the variables,
or of the pronouns. Various turns of phrase in ordinary language that seemed to invoke novel sorts of objects may disappear under such regimentation. At other points new ontic
commitments may emerge. There is room for choice, and
one chooses with a view to simplicity in one's overall system
of the world.

More objects are wanted, certainly, than just bodies and
substances. We need all sorts of parts or portions of substances. For lack of a definable stopping place, the natural
course at this point is to admit as an object the material content of any portion of space-time, however irregular and discontinuous and heterogeneous. This is the generalization of
the primitive and ill-defined category of bodies to what I call
physical objects.

Substances themselves fall into place now as physical objects. Milk, or wood, or sugar, is the discontinuous four-
dimensional physical object comprising all the world's milk,
or wood, or sugar, ever.

The reasons for taking the physical objects thus spatio-
temporally, and treating time on a par with space, are overwhelming and have been adequately noted in various places.[2]
Let us pass over them and ponder rather the opposition to
the four-dimensional view; for it is a curiosity worth looking into. Part of the opposition is obvious misinterpretation:
the notion that time is stopped, change is denied, and all is
frozen eternally in a fourth dimension. These are the misgivings of unduly nervous folk who overestimate the power
of words. Time as a fourth dimension is still time, and differences along the fourth dimension are still changes; they
are merely treated more simply and efficiently than they
otherwise might be.

Opposition has proceeded also from the venerable doctrine
that not all the statements about the future have truth

2. E.g., in my *Word and Object*, pp. 170ff.

values now, because some of them remain, as of now, causally undetermined. Properly viewed, however, determinism is beside the point. The question of future truths is a matter of verbal convenience and is as innocuous as Doris Day's tautological fatalism "Che sarà sarà."

Another question that has been similarly linked to determinism, wrongly and notoriously, is that of freedom of the will. Like Spinoza, Hume, and so many others, I count an act as free insofar as the agent's motives or drives are a link in its causal chain. Those motives or drives may themselves be as rigidly determined as you please.

It is for me an ideal of pure reason to subscribe to determinism as fully as the quantum physicists will let me. But there are well-known difficulties in the way of rigorously formulating it. When we say of some event that it is determined by present ones, shall we mean that there is a general conditional, true but perhaps unknown to us, whose antecedent is instantiated by present events and whose consequent is instantiated by the future event in question? Without some drastic limitations on complexity and vocabulary, determinism so defined is pretty sure to boil down to "Che sarà sarà" and to afford at best a great idea for a song. Yet the idea in all its vagueness retains validity as an ideal of reason. It is valid as a general injunction: look for mechanisms.

This has been quite a spray, or spree, of philosophical miscellany. Let us now return to our cabbages, which is to say, our newly generalized physical objects. One of the benefits that the generalization confers is the accommodation of events as objects. An action or transaction can be identified with the physical objects consisting of the temporal segment or segments of the agent or agents for the duration. Misgivings about this approach to events have been expressed, on the grounds that it does not distinguish two acts that are performed simultaneously, such as walking and chewing gum. But I think that all the distinctions that need to be drawn can be drawn, still, at the level of general terms. Not all walks are gum chewings, nor vice versa, even though an occasional one may be. Some things may be said of an act on the score of its being a walk, and distinctive things may be said of it on the score of its being a chewing of gum, even though it be accounted one and the same event. There are its crural features on the one hand and its maxillary features on the other.

A reason for being particularly glad to have accommodated events is Davidson's logic of adverbs,[3] for Davidson has shown to my satisfaction that quantification over events is far and away the best way of construing adverbial constructions.

Our liberal notion of physical objects brings out an important point about identity. Some philosophers propound puzzles as to what to say about personal identity in cases of split personality or in fantasies about metempsychosis or brain transplants. These are not questions about the nature of identity. They are questions about how we might best construe the term 'person'. Again there is the stock example of the ship of Theseus, rebuilt bit by bit until no original bit remained. Whether we choose to reckon it still as the same ship is a question not of 'same' but of 'ship'; a question of how we choose to individuate that term over time.

Any coherent general term has its own principle of individuation, its own criterion of identity among its denotata. Often the principle is vague, as the principle of individuation of persons is shown to be by the science-fiction examples; and a term is as vague as its principle of individuation.

Most of our general terms individuate by continuity considerations, because continuity favors causal connections. But even useful terms, grounded in continuity, often diverge in their individuation, as witness the evolving ship of Theseus, on the one hand, and its original substance, gradually dispersed, on the other. Continuity follows both branches.

All this should have been clear without help of our liberal notion of physical object, but this notion drives the point home. It shows how empty it would be to ask, out of context, whether a certain glimpse yesterday and a certain glimpse today were glimpses of the same thing. They may or may not have been glimpses of the same body, but they certainly were glimpses of *a* same thing, a same physical object; for the con-

3. "The logical form of action sentences."

tent of any portion of space-time, however miscellaneously scattered in space and time that portion be, counts as a physical object.

The president or presidency of the United States is one such physical object, though not a body. It is a spatially discontinuous object made up of temporal segments, each of which is a temporal stage also of a body, a human one. The whole thing has its temporal beginning in 1789, when George Washington took office, and its end only at the final takeover, quite possibly more than two centuries later. Another somewhat similar physical object is the Dalai Lama, an example that has been invigorated by a myth of successive reincarnation. But the myth is unnecessary.

A body is a special kind of physical object, one that is roughly continuous spatially and rather chunky and that contrasts abruptly with most of its surroundings and is individuated over time by continuity of displacement, distortion, and discoloration. These are vague criteria, especially so in view of molecular theory, which teaches that the boundary of a solid is ill defined and that the continuity of a solid is only apparent and properly a matter of degree.

The step of generalization from body to physical object follows naturally, we saw, on the reification of portions of stuff. It follows equally naturally on molecular theory: if even a solid is diffuse, why stop there?

We can be happy not to have to rest existence itself on the vague notions of body and substance, as we would have to do if bodies and substances were our whole ontology. Specific individuatives such as 'dog' or 'desk' continue, like 'body', to suffer from vagueness on the score of the microphysical boundaries of their denotata, as well as vagueness on the score of marginal denotata themselves, such as makeshift desks and remote ancestors of dogs; but all this is vagueness only of classification and not of existence. All the variants qualify as physical objects.

Physical objects in this generous sense constitute a fairly lavish universe, but more is wanted—notably numbers. Measurement is useful in cookery and commerce, and in the fullness of time it rises to a nobler purpose: the formulation of quantitative laws. These are the mainstay of scientific theory,[4] and they call upon the full resources of the real numbers. Diagonals call for irrationals, circumferences call for transcendentals. Nor can we rest with constants; we must quantify over numbers. Admitting numbers as values of variables means reifying them and recognizing numerals as names of them; and this is required for the sake of generality in our quantitative laws.

Measures have sometimes been viewed as impure numbers: nine miles, nine gallons. We do better to follow Carnap[5] in construing each scale of measurement as a polyadic general term relating physical objects to pure numbers. Thus 'gallon xy' means that the presumably fluid and perhaps scatterd physical object x amounts to y gallons, and 'mile xyz' means that the physical objects x and y are z miles apart. Pure numbers, then, apparently belong in our ontology.

Classes do too, for whenever we count things we measure a class. If a statistical generality about populations quantifies over numbers of people, it has to quantify also over the classes whose numbers those are. Quantification over classes figures also in other equally inconspicuous ways, as witness Frege's familiar definition of ancestor in terms of parent: one's ancestors are the members shared by every class that contains oneself and the parents of its members.

Sometimes in natural science we are concerned explicitly with classes, or seem to be—notably in taxonomy. We read that there are over a quarter-million species of beetles. Here evidently we are concerned with a quarter-million classes and, over and above these, a class of all these clasess. However, we can economize here. Instead of talking of species in this context, we can make do with a dyadic general term applicable to beetles: 'conspecific'. To say that there are over a quarter-million species is equivalent to saying that there is a class of over a quarter-million *beetles* none of which are conspecific. This still conveys impressive information, and it still requires reification of a big class, but a class only of beetles and not of classes.

4. See Essay 18, below.
5. *Physikalische Begriffsbildung.*

This way of dodging a class of classes is not always available. It worked here because species are mutually exclusive.

Note the purely auxiliary role of classes in all three examples. In counting things we are more interested in the things counted than in their class. In the genealogical example the concern is with people, their parentage and ancestry; classes entered only in deriving the one from the other. In the example of the beetles, classes were indeed out in the open—even inordinately so, I argued. But even so, it is because of an interest still strictly in beetles, not classes, that one says there are so many species. The statement tells us that beetles are highly discriminate in their mating. It conveys this sort of information, but more precisely, and it makes auxiliary reference to classes as a means of doing so. Limited to physical objects though our interests be, an appeal to classes can thus be instrumental in pursuing those interests. I look upon mathematics in general in the same way, in its relation to natural science. But to view classes, numbers, and the rest in this instrumental way is not to deny having reified them; it is only to explain why.

III

So we assume abstract objects over and above the physical objects. For a better grasp of what this means, let us consider a simple case: the natural numbers. The conditions we need to impose on them are simple and few: we need to assume an object as first number and an operator that yields a unique new number whenever applied to a number. In short, we need a progression. Any progression will do, for the following reasons. The fundamental use of natural numbers is in measuring classes: in saying that a class has n members. Other serious uses prove to be reducible to this use. But any progression will serve *this* purpose; for we can say that a class has n members by saying that its members are in correlation with the members of the progression up to n—not caring which progression it may be.

There are ways of defining specific progressions of classes, no end of ways. When we feel the need of natural numbers we can simply reach for members of one of these progres-

sions instead—whichever one comes handy. On the basis of
natural numbers, in turn, it is possible with the help of
classes to define the ratios and the irrational numbers in
well-known ways. On one such construction they turn out
to be simply certain classes of natural numbers. So, when
we feel the need of ratios and irrationals, we can simply
reach for appropriate subclasses of one of the progressions
of classes. We need never talk of numbers, though in practice it is convenient to carry over the numerical jargon.

Numbers, then, except as a manner of speaking, are by
the board. We have physical objects and we have classes. Not
just classes of physical objects, but classes of classes and
so on up. Some of these higher levels are needed to do the
work of numbers and other gear of applied mathematics,
and one then assumes the whole hierarchy if only for want
of a natural stopping place.

But now what are classes? Consider the bottom layer, the
classes of physical objects. Every relative clause or other
general term determines a class, the class of those physical
objects of which the term can be truly predicated. Two terms
determine the same class of physical objects just in case the
terms are true of just the same physical objects. Still, com-
patibly with all this we could reconstrue every class systematically as its complement and then compensate for the
switch by reinterpreting the dyadic general term 'member
of' to mean what had been meant by 'not a member of'. The
effects would cancel and one would never know.

We thus seem to see a profound difference between abstract objects and concrete ones. A physical object, one feels,
can be pinned down by pointing—in many cases, anyway,
and to a fair degree. But I am persuaded that this contrast
is illusory.

By way of example, consider again my liberalized notion
of a physical object as the material content of any place-
time, any portion of space-time. This was an intuitive explanation, intending no reification of space-time itself. But
we could just as well reify those portions of space-time and
treat of them instead of the physical objects. Or, indeed, call
them physical objects. Whatever can be said from the old
point of view can be paraphrased to suit the new point of

view, with no effect on the structure of scientific theory or on its links with observational evidence. Wherever we had a predication '*x* is a *P*', said of a physical object *x*, we would in effect read '*x* is the place-time of a *P*'; actually we would just reinterpret the old '*P*' as 'place-time of a *P*', and rewrite nothing.

Space separately, or place anyway, is an untenable notion. If there were really places, there would be absolute rest and absolute motion; for change of place would be absolute motion. However, there is no such objection to place-times or space-time.

If we accept a redundant ontology containing both physical objects and place-times, then we can indeed declare them distinct; but even then, if we switch the physical objects with their place-times and then compensate by reinterpreting the dyadic general term 'is the material content of' to mean 'is the place-time of' and vice versa, no one can tell the difference. We could choose either interpretation indifferently if we were translating from an unrelated language.

These last examples are unnatural, for they work only if the empty place-times are repudiated and just the full ones are admitted as values of the variables. If we were seriously to reconstrue physical objects as place-times, we would surely enlarge our universe to include the empty ones and thus gain the simplicity of a continuous system of coordinates.

This change in ontology, the abandonment of physical objects in favor of pure space-time, proves to be more than a contrived example. The elementary particles have been wavering alarmingly as physics progresses. Situations arise that curiously challenge the individuality of a particle, not only over time, but even at a single time. A field theory in which states are ascribed directly to place-times may well present a better picture, and some physicists think it does.

At this point a further transfer of ontology suggests itself: we can drop the space-time regions in favor of the corresponding classes of quadruples of numbers according to an arbitrarily adopted system of coordinates. We are left with just the ontology of pure set theory, since the numbers and their quadruples can be modeled within it. There are no longer any physical objects to serve as individuals at the base of the hierarchy of classes, but there is no harm in that. It is common practice in set theory nowadays to start merely with the null class, form its unit class, and so on, thus generating an infinite lot of classes, from which all the usual luxuriance of further infinites can be generated.

One may object to thus identifying the world with the output of so arbitrarily chosen a system of coordinates. On the other hand, one may condone this on the ground that no numerically specific coordinates will appear in the laws of truly theoretical physics, thanks to the very arbitrariness of the coordinates. The specificity of the coordinates would make itself known only when one descends to coarser matters of astronomy, geography, geology, and history, and here it is perhaps appropriate.

We have now looked at three cases in which we interpret or reinterpret one domain of objects by identifying it with part of another domain. In the first example, numbers were identified with some of the classes in one way or another. In the second example, physical objects were identified with some of the place-times, namely, the full ones. In the third example, place-times were identified with some of the classes, namely, classes of quadruples of numbers. In each such case simplicity is gained, if to begin with we had been saddled with the two domains.

There is a fourth example of the same thing that is worth noting, for it concerns the long-debated dualism of mind and body. I hardly need say that the dualism is unattractive. If mind and body are to interact, we are at a loss for a plausible mechanism to the purpose. Also we are faced with the melancholy office of talking physicists out of their cherished conservation laws. On the other hand, an aseptic dualistic parallelism is monumentally redundant, a monument to everything multiplicacious that William of Ockham so rightly deplored. But now it is easily seen that dualism with or without interaction is reducible to physical monism, unless disembodied spirits are assumed. For the dualist who rejects disembodied spirits is bound to agree that for every state of mind there is an exactly concurrent and readily specifiable state of the accompanying body. Readily specifiable certainly; the bodily state is specifiable simply as the state of accompanying a mind that is in that mental state. But then we can settle for the bodily states outright, bypassing the mental states in terms of which I specified them. We can just reinterpret the mentalistic terms as denoting these correlated bodily states, and who is to know the difference?

This reinterpretation of mentalistic terms is reminiscent of the treatment of events that I suggested earlier, and it raises the same question of discrimination of concurrent events. But I would just propose again the answer that I gave then.

I take it as evident that there is no inverse option here, no hope of sustaining mental monism by assigning mental states to all states of physical objects.

These four cases of reductive reinterpretation are gratifying, enabling us as they do to dispense with one of two domains and make do with the other alone. But I find the other sort of reinterpretation equally instructive, the sort where we save nothing but merely change or seem to change our objects without disturbing either the structure or the empirical support of a scientific theory in the slightest. All that is needed in either case, clearly, is a rule whereby a unique object of the supposedly new sort is assigned to each of the old objects. I call such a rule a proxy function. Then, instead of predicating a general term '*P*' of an old object *x*, saying that *x* is a *P*, we reinterpret *x* as a new object and say that it is the *f* of a *P*, where '*f*' expresses the proxy function. Instead of saying that *x* is a dog, we say that *x* is the lifelong filament of space-time taken up by a dog. Or, really, we just adhere to the old term '*P*', 'dog', and reinterpret it as '*f* of a *P*', 'place-time of a dog'. This is the strategy that we have seen in various examples.

The apparent change is twofold and sweeping. The original objects have been supplanted and the general terms reinterpreted. There has been a revision of ontology on the one hand and of ideology, so to say, on the other; they go together. Yet verbal behavior proceeds undisturbed, warranted by the same observations as before and elicited by the same observations. Nothing really has changed.

The conclusion I draw is the inscrutability of reference.

To say what objects someone is talking about is to say no more than how we propose to translate his terms into ours; we are free to vary the decision with a proxy function. The translation adopted arrests the free-floating reference of the alien terms only relatively to the free-floating reference of our own terms, by linking the two.

The point is not that we ourselves are casting about in vain for a mooring. Staying aboard our own language and not rocking the boat, we are borne smoothly along on it and all is well; 'rabbit' denotes rabbits, and there is no sense in asking 'Rabbits in what sense of "rabbit"?' Reference goes inscrutable if, rocking the boat, we contemplate a permutational mapping of our language on itself, or if we undertake translation.

Structure is what matters to a theory, and not the choice of its objects. F. P. Ramsey urged this point fifty years ago, arguing along other lines, and in a vague way it had been a persistent theme also in Russell's *Analysis of Matter*. But Ramsey and Russell were talking only of what they called theoretical objects, as opposed to observable objects.

I extend the doctrine to objects generally, for I see all objects as theoretical. This is a consequence of taking seriously the insight that I traced from Bentham—namely, the semantic primacy of sentences. It is occasion sentences, not terms, that are to be seen as conditioned to stimulations. Even our primordial objects, bodies, are already theoretical —most conspicuously so when we look to their individuation over time. Whether we encounter the same apple the next time around, or only another one like it, is settled if at all by inference from a network of hypotheses that we have internalized little by little in the course of acquiring the non-observational superstructure of our language.

It is occasion sentences that report the observations on which science rests. The scientific output is likewise sentential: true sentences, we hope, truths about nature. The objects, or values of variables, serve merely as indices along the way, and we may permute or supplant them as we please as long as the sentence-to-sentence structure is preserved. The scientific system, ontology and all, is a conceptual bridge of our own making, linking sensory stimulation to sensory stimulation. I am repeating what I said at the beginning.

But I also expressed, at the beginning, my unswerving belief in external things—people, nerve endings, sticks, stones. This I reaffirm. I believe also, if less firmly, in atoms and electrons and in classes. Now how is all this robust realism to be reconciled with the barren scene that I have just been depicting? The answer is naturalism: the recognition that it is within science itself, and not in some prior philosophy, that reality is to be identified and described.

The semantical considerations that seemed to undermine all this were concerned not with assessing reality but with analyzing method and evidence. They belong not to ontology but to the methodology of ontology, and thus to epistemology. Those considerations showed that I could indeed turn my back on my external things and classes and ride the proxy functions to something strange and different without doing violence to any evidence. But all ascription of reality must come rather from within one's theory of the world; it is incoherent otherwise.

My methodological talk of proxy functions and inscrutability of reference must be seen as naturalistic too; it likewise is no part of a first philosophy prior to science. The setting is still the physical world, seen in terms of the global science to which, with minor variations, we all subscribe. Amid all this there are our sensory receptors and the bodies near and far whose emanations impinge on our receptors. Epistemology, for me, or what comes nearest to it, is the study of how we animals can have contrived that very science, given just that sketchy neural input. It is this study that reveals that displacements of our ontology through proxy functions would have measured up to that neural input no less faithfully. To recognize this is not to repudiate the ontology in terms of which the recognition took place.

We *can* repudiate it. We are free to switch, without doing violence to any evidence. If we switch, then this epistemological remark itself undergoes appropriate reinterpretation too; nerve endings and other things give way to appropriate proxies, again without straining any evidence. But it is a confusion to suppose that we can stand aloof and recognize all the alternative ontologies as true in their several ways, all the envisaged worlds as real. It is a confusion of truth with evidential support. Truth is immanent, and there is no higher. We must speak from within a theory, albeit any of various.

Transcendental argument, or what purports to be first philosophy, tends generally to take on rather this status of immanent epistemology insofar as I succeed in making sense of it. What evaporates is the transcendental question of the reality of the external world—the question whether or in how far our science measures up to the *Ding an sich*.

Our scientific theory can indeed go wrong, and precisely in the familiar way: through failure of predicted observation. But what if, happily and unbeknownst, we have achieved a theory that is conformable to every possible observation, past and future? In what sense could the world then be said to deviate from what the theory claims? Clearly in none, even if we can somehow make sense of the phrase 'every possible observation'. Our overall scientific theory demands of the world only that it be so structured as to assure the sequences of stimulation that our theory gives us to expect. More concrete demands are empty, what with the freedom of proxy functions.

Radical skepticism stems from the sort of confusion I have alluded to, but is not of itself incoherent. Science is vulnerable to illusion on its own showing, what with seemingly bent sticks in water and the like, and the skeptic may be seen merely as overreacting when he repudiates science across the board. Experience might still take a turn that would justify his doubts about external objects. Our success in predicting observations might fall off sharply, and concomitantly with this we might begin to be somewhat successful in basing predictions upon dreams or reveries. At that point we might reasonably doubt our theory of nature in even fairly broad outlines. But our doubts would still be immanent, and of a piece with the scientific endeavor.

My attitude toward the project of a rational reconstruction of the world from sense data is similarly naturalistic. I do not regard the project as incoherent, though its motivation in some cases is confused. I see it as a project of positing a realm of entities intimately related to the stimulation of the sensory surfaces, and then, with the help perhaps of an auxiliary realm of entities in set theory, proceeding by contextual definition to construct a language adequate to natural science. It is an attractive idea, for it would bring scientific discourse into a much more explicit and systematic relation to its observational checkpoints. My only reservation is that I am convinced, regretfully, that it cannot be done.

Another notion that I would take pains to rescue from the abyss of the transcendental is the notion of a matter of fact. A place where the notion proves relevant is in connection with my doctrine of the indeterminacy of translation. I have argued that two conflicting manuals of translation can both do justice to all dispositions to behavior, and that, in such a case, there is no fact of the matter of which manual is right. The intended notion of matter of fact is not transcendental or yet epistemological, not even a question of evidence; it is ontological, a question of reality, and to be taken naturalistically within our scientific theory of the world. Thus suppose, to make things vivid, that we are settling still for a physics of elementary particles and recognizing a dozen or so basic states and relations in which they may stand. Then when I say there is no fact of the matter, as regards, say, the two rival manuals of translation, what I mean is that both manuals are compatible with all the same distributions of states and relations over elementary particles. In a word, they are physically equivalent. Needless to say, there is no presumption of our being able to sort out the pertinent distributions of microphysical states and relations. I speak of a physical condition and not an empirical criterion.

It is in the same sense that I say there is no fact of the matter of our interpreting any man's ontology in one way or, via proxy functions, in another. Any man's, that is to say, except ourselves. We can switch our own ontology too without doing violence to any evidence, but in so doing we switch from our elementary particles to some manner of proxies and thus reinterpret our standard of what counts as a fact of the matter. Factuality, like gravitation and electric charge, is internal to our theory of nature.

2

✒ *Empirical Content*

The preceding essay was concerned with the empirical significance of the assuming of objects. This one is concerned,
yet more abstractly, with empirical significance as such:
with the relation of scientific theory to its sensory evidence.
As before, my stance is naturalistic. By sensory evidence I
mean stimulation of sensory receptors. I accept our prevail-
ing physical theory and therewith the physiology of my
receptors, and then proceed to speculate on how this sensory
input supports the very physical theory that I am accepting.
I do not claim thereby to be proving the physical theory, so
there is no vicious circle.

What sort of thing is a scientific theory? It is an idea, one
might naturally say, or a complex of ideas. But the most
practical way of coming to grips with ideas, and usually the
only way, is by way of the words that express them. What
to look for in the way of theories, then, are the sentences
that express them. There will be no need to decide what a
theory is or when to regard two sets of sentences as formulations of the same theory; we can just talk of the theory
formulations as such.

The relation to be analyzed, then, is the relation between
our sensory stimulations and our scientific theory formulations: the relation between the physicist's sentences on the

---

This piece is adapted from a paper, "Gegenstand und Beobachtung,"
that I am to present at Stuttgart in June 1981. There are echoes in it
of "On empirically equivalent systems of the world."

one hand, treating of gravitation and electrons and the like, and on the other hand the triggering of his sensory receptors.

Let us begin by looking at the sentences most directly connected with sensory stimulation. These are the occasion sentences noted in the preceding essay. They are occasion sentences of a special sort, which I call *observation* sentences. By this I do not mean to suggest that they are about observation, or sense data, or stimulation. Examples are 'It's raining', 'It's milk', as before. An observation sentence is an occasion sentence that the speaker will consistently assent to when his sensory receptors are stimulated in certain ways, and consistently dissent from when they are stimulated in certain other ways. If querying the sentence elicits assent from the given speaker on one occasion, it will elicit assent likewise on any other occasion when the same total set of receptors is triggered; and similarly for dissent. This and this only is what qualifies sentences as observation sentences for the speaker in question, and this is the sense in which they are the sentences most directly associated with sensory stimulation.

Naturally the exact same total set of sensory receptors is unlikely to be triggered twice. The more nearly it is approximated, however, the likelier the assent or dissent should be. Naturally, moreover, many of the receptors will be irrelevant to any particular sentence; but this excess is harmless, canceling out. Only the relevant receptors will be triggered on *all* the occasions appropriate to the sentence in question.

The notion of observation sentence can be further refined by allowing for degrees of observationality. Hesitation can then be taken into account. But it is already evident from what I have said that a pretty substantial notion of observation sentence is before us here, despite latter-day skepticism on the subject.

The problem of relating theory to sensory stimulation may now be put less forbiddingly as that of relating theory formulations to observation sentences. In this we have a head start in that we recognize the observation sentences to be theory-laden. What this means is that terms embedded in observation sentences recur in the theory formulations.

What qualifies a sentence as observational is not a lack of such terms, but just that the sentence taken as an undivided whole commands assent consistently or dissent consistently when the same global sensory stimulation is repeated. What relates the observation sentence to theory, on the other hand, is the sharing of embedded terms.

When we proceed to look for inferential connections between observation sentences and theory formulations, however, we are caught up in a succession of problems. Problem 1: observation sentences are occasion sentences, whereas theory is formulated in *eternal* sentences, true or false once for all. What logical connection can there be between the two? Evidently we need first to eternalize the observation sentence. Thus a given utterance of 'It's raining' might be eternalized to read 'Raining at 42°N and 71°W on March 9, 1981, at 0500'. We thus run headlong into Problem 2, the problem of determining places and times on an observational basis. Even if we were to postpone the sophistication of latitude and longitude by starting rather with place names, we would still need to explain how to determine by name where we are at the time and, indeed, how to determine the date and time of day.

However, suppose for the moment that Problem 2 were solved. Suppose the eternalized reports of observation were available. Still we cannot expect scientific theory to imply such sentences outright. Science normally predicts observations only on the assumption of initial conditions. We arrange an observable situation and then, if our scientific theory is right, a predicted further observation ensues. What a scientific theory implies is thus not an eternalized observation sentence outright, but rather a conditional sentence, what I have called an *observation conditional*.[1] It is a sentence ⌜If ϕ then ψ⌝ where ψ is an eternalized observation sentence and ϕ states the initial conditions. Since the initial conditions are to be observable too, ϕ will also be an eternalized observation sentence; or perhaps it will be a conjunction of several, since they may differ from one another in respect of the places and times.

---

1. "On empirically equivalent systems of the world."

This brings us to Problem 3. The initial conditions expressed in ϕ refer to times and places at some remove from those referred to in ψ; perhaps at various removes. In allowing this we are stopping short of fundamentals. We are allowing a certain amount of unchecked theory to slip through the net. At the place-time where the predicted observation is due, how does the experimenter know that the supposed initial conditions were fulfilled a while back and some way off? He can have only indirect evidence of this: his memory, his notes, the testimony of others. These are after-effects, from which those past arrangements are inferred. The inference is already a part of scientific theory, however tacit and unconscious. Strictly, all the experimenter has to go on are his present observations. They are paired. One is the immediate initial condition, which may be the present evidence of various past initial conditions ordinarily so called. The other is the predicted observation.

Clearly, then, our observation conditions were too liberal. We should limit our attention to conditional sentences ⌜If ϕ then ψ⌝ where ϕ and ψ stand for eternalized observation sentences referring to one and the same place-time.

Having thus disposed of Problem 3, let us recall Problem 2: the problem of specifying and determining places and times on an observational basis. There is an easy step that bypasses this problem, now that we have required the observation conditional to refer to the same place-time in both its clauses. Namely, we can now dispense with the specification of a place-time and claim, instead, generality. We can withdraw to what I may call *observation categoricals*—sentences like 'Where there is smoke there is fire' or 'When it rains it pours' or 'When night falls the lamps are lit'. These enjoy generality over places and times, but they do not need to be read as assuming a prior ontology of places and times or any implicit universal quantification over them. The construction can be seen rather as a simple one, learned early. The child may learn the component observation sentences 'Here is smoke' and 'Here is fire' by ostension, and then the compound is an eternal sentence that expresses his having become conditioned to associate the one with the other.

The problem of places and times, Problem 2, is thus circumvented. Specifications of place-times are still indispensable to science, but we have kicked them upstairs: we have consigned them to the network of theoretical concepts where they belong, at a comfortable remove from observation.

Here, then, is further progress in relating scientific theory to its sensory evidence. The relation consists in the implying of true observation categoricals by the theory formulation. And how do we know when an observation categorical is true? We never do, conclusively, by observation, because each is general. But observation can falsify an observation categorical. We may observe night falling and the lamps not being lit. We may observe smoke and find no fire.

This characterization fits Popper's dictum that scientific theories can only be refuted, never established. But we do see scope still for intuitive support of theories. An observation categorical gains our confidence as our observations continue to conform to it without exception; this is simple habit formation, or conditioning. A theory formulation, in turn, gains our confidence as the observation categoricals implied by it retain our confidence.

The observation categoricals implied by a theory formulation constitute, we may say, its empirical content; for it is only the observation categoricals that link theory to observation. If two theory formulations imply all the same observation categoricals, they are empirically equivalent.

A theory formulation merely implies its observation categoricals, and is not implied by them, unless it is trivial. Two theory formulations may thus imply all the same observation conditionals without implying each other. They can be empirically equivalent without being logically equivalent.

In fact, they can be empirically equivalent and yet logically inconsistent, incompatible. We can get a trivial example of this situation by simply switching two words that do not appear in any observation sentences—perhaps the words 'molecule' and 'electron'. Thus imagine an exhaustive encyclopedic formulation of our total scientific theory of the world. Imagine also another just like it except that the words 'molecule' and 'electron' are switched. The formulations are empirically equivalent: all the implicative connections between the observation categoricals and the sentences containing the word 'molecule' or 'electron' in the one theory formulation are matched by the same implicative connections in the other theory with the two words rewritten. The observation categoricals remain identical, for they lack those words. Yet the two theory formulations are logically incompatible, for the one attributes properties to molecules that the other formulation *denies* of molecules and attributes to electrons. (I am indebted here to Humphries.)

The natural response to this trivial example is that the two formulations are really formulations of the same theory in slightly different words, and that the one can be translated into the other by switching the two words back. More generally, whenever we find terms, extraneous to the observation categoricals themselves, that can be so reinterpreted throughout one of the theory formulations as to reconcile it with the other theory formulation, and not disturb the empirical content, we see the conflict to be superficial and uninteresting.

Suppose, however, two empirically equivalent theory formulations that we see no way of reconciling by such a reinterpretation of terms. We probably would not know that they are empirically equivalent, for the usual way of finding them so would be by hitting upon such a reinterpretation. Still, we might succeed somehow in persuading ourselves of the empirical equivalence of the two formulations despite finding no way of intertranslation. Then we should indeed recognize the two as equally well *warranted*. We might even oscillate between them, for the sake of a richer perspective on nature. But we should still limit the ascription of truth to whichever theory formulation we are entertaining at the time, for there is no wider frame of reference.[2]

I suggested that the empirical content of a theory formulation consists of its observation categoricals. This definition is appealing in its catholicity. Observation sentences enter it holophrastically, with no regard to internal structure beyond what may go into the logical links of implication between theory formulations and observation categoricals. The language need not be bivalent, it need not be realistic, it need

2. This paragraph departs from earlier printings.

not even have anything clearly recognizable as terms or as reference, or any recognizable ontology. The one grammatical construction that we need specifically to recognize is the one that combines observation sentences two by two into observation categoricals. Since this construction has the very primitive effect of expressing conditioned expectations, something to the purpose doubtless exists in any language, however exotic.

3

✒ *What Price Bivalence?*

A good scientific theory is under tension from two oppos-
ing forces: the drive for evidence and the drive for system.
Theoretical terms should be subject to observable criteria,
the more the better, and the more directly the better, other
things being equal; and they should lend themselves to systematic laws, the simpler the better, other things being
equal. If either of these drives were unchecked by the other,
it would issue in something unworthy of the name of scientific theory: in the one case a mere record of observations,
and in the other a myth without foundation.

What we settle for, if I may switch my metaphor from
dynamics to economics, is a trade-off. We gain simplicity of
theory, within reason, by recourse to terms that relate only
indirectly, intermittently, and rather tenuously to observation. The values that we thus trade off one against the other
—evidential value and systematic value—are incommensur-
able. Scientists of different philosophical temper will differ
in how much dilution of evidence they are prepared to accept
for a given systematic benefit, and vice versa. Such was the
difference between Ernst Mach and the atomists. Such is the
difference between the intuitionists and the communicants
of classical logic. Such is the difference between the Copen-
hagen school of quantum physicists and the proponents of
hidden variables. Those who prize the evidential side more
are the readier to gerrymander their language in such ways

Reprinted from the *Journal of Philosophy* 78 (1981), with additions.

as to excise one or another sheaf of undecidable sentences, even though without hope of excising all. Those who prize the systematic side more are the readier to round language out, gaining smoothness and tolerating, to that end, some increment of adipose tissue.

We stalwarts of two-valued logic buy its sweet simplicity at no small price in respect of the harboring of undecidables. We declare that it is either true or false that there was an odd number of blades of grass in Harvard Yard at the dawn of Commencement Day, 1903. The matter is undecidable, but we maintain that there is a fact of the matter. Similarly for countless similar trivialities. Similarly for more extravagant undecidables, such as whether there was a hydrogen atom within a meter of some remote point that we may specify by space-time coordinates. And similarly, on the mathematical side, for the continuum hypothesis or the question of the existence of inaccessible cardinals. Bivalence is, as Dummett argues (pp. 145–165), the hallmark of realism.

I propose in the present pages neither to defend bivalence nor to repudiate it. My inclination is to adhere to it for the simplicity of theory that it affords, but my purpose now is to acknowledge the costs.

Besides the realists's undecidable matters of fact, with respect to physical objects or infinite cardinal numbers, there is also the vagueness of terms to reckon with; and bivalence raises issues also in this domain. The culmination of these latter troubles is the sorites paradox, the ancient paradox of the heap. If removal of a single grain from a heap always leaves a heap, then, by mathematical induction, removal of all the grains leaves a heap. Russell's latter-day version is no less familiar: if the loss of a hair renders no man bald, then neither does the loss of any number of them. Bivalence seals the paradox, requiring as it does at each stage that the statement that a heap remains, or that the man is bald, be univocally true or false.

The paradox is engendered by vague terms generally. Moreover, as Crispin Wright points out, a term is apt to be vague if it is to be learned by ostension, since its applicability must admit of being judged on the spot and so cannot hinge on fine distinctions laboriously drawn. Exceptions to this can be contrived, as by Dummett (p. 265), but still the evident moral is that we are deep in contradiction before we finish acquiring the bare ostensive beginnings of cognitive language.

What saves us is that at that stage we are too naive to appreciate our predicament; mathematical induction is a theoretical adjunct, not yet acquired. When we do reach the point of positing numbers and plying their laws, then is the time to heed the contradictions and to take steps. One expedient that often serves is abandonment of a vague absolute term in favor of a relative term of comparison. The expedient is familiar in the case of such terms as 'big', 'tall', and 'heavy', and it works equally for 'bald': we may abandon 'bald' in favor of 'balder than'. The case of 'heap' is somewhat more awkward, however, and 'mountain' yet more so. Here the clearer course is to keep the absolute term but to resolve its vagueness by arbitrary stipulations.

'Mountain' affords a rich example, for there is the vagueness of acceptable altitude, the vagueness of boundary at the base, and the consequent indecision as to when to count two summits as two mountains and when as one. Possible stipulations are as follows. Leaving foreign planets conveniently aside, we may define a mountain as any region of the earth's surface such that (a) the boundary is of uniform altitude, (b) the highest point, or one of them, is at an inclination of at least ten degrees above every boundary point and twenty degrees above some, and is at least a thousand feet above them, and (c) the region is part of no other region fulfilling (a) and (b). (Theorem: the boundary of a mountain is the outermost contour line that lies wholly within ten degrees of steepness from the summit and partly within twenty.)

It is in this spirit that what had been learned as observation terms may be redefined, on pain of paradox, as theoretical terms whose application may depend in marginal cases on protracted tests and indirect inferences. The sorites paradox is one imperative reason for precision in science, along with more familiar reasons.

Not that it is customary in general to devise such precise criteria. Partial steps are taken as needed, and the tacit fic-

tion is adopted that other terms are subject to precise limits
that we are not bothering to settle. Some terms are adopted
from observation language and incorporated into scientific
language with their edges refined, others are incorporated
as if refined; and sufficient unto the day is the evil thereof.
We are thus enabled to make do with our bivalent logic and
our smooth and simple arithemetic, including mathematical
induction.

To take this attitude is merely to recognize and acquiesce
in what Waismann called the open texture of empirical
terms. To reason *as if* our terms were precise seems pretty
straightforward as long as we see that they could be made
precise by arbitrary stipulations whenever occasion might
arise. However, Unger has lately argued that the problem
runs deeper. Diminish a table, conceptually, molecule by
molecule: when is a table not a table? No stipulations will
avail us here, however arbitrary.

Each removal of a molecule leaves a physical object, yes, in
my liberal sense of the term—namely, the material content
of a portion of space-time. A table contains a graded multitude of nested or overlapping physical objects each of which
embodies enough of the substance to have qualified as a table
in its own right, but only in abstraction from the rest of the
molecules. Each of these physical objects would qualify as a
table, that is, if cleared of the overlying and surrounding
molecules, but should not be counted as a table when still
embedded in a further physical object that so qualifies in
turn; for tables are meant to be mutually exclusive. Only
the outermost, the sum of this nest of physical objects, counts
as a table.

Yet something remains of Unger's point. There remains
the question how much to include in the table in the way of
superficial or hovering molecules. We cannot simply rule that
the table passes muster both with and without various of the
marginal molecules, for, again, tables are mutually exclusive; only one is present. Now this case differs from the
ancient example of the heap, or the example of baldness, in
that we cannot settle the demarcation of the table even by an
arbitrary ruling. We were able to stipulate an arbitrary
minimum to the number of grains in a heap, and a maximum

to the numbers of hairs on a bald head, but we are at a loss to frame a convention for the molecular demarcation of the surface of a table. Words fail us.

The question about the grass of 1903 hinged, one felt, on a robust matter of fact. Still, being clearly undecidable, the question makes empirical sense to us only by analogy and extrapolation. It makes sense because we often do count things, and are prepared even to count present blades of grass. We project these vivid notions into the inaccessible past as a matter of course, such is the organization of our system of the world. The physicist has done more of the same, and only more extravagantly, in giving us the makings of our idle question about the hydrogen atom. This undecidable question, like the one about the grass, makes empirical sense to us only by virtue of the devious connections between our systematic theory of the world and the various observations to which the system as a whole is answerable. The connections are more complex and more tenuous in this case of the hydrogen atom than in the case of the grass of 1903, but the question is still, for the bivalent-minded, a question of objective fact.

One has a different feeling about the question of the heap, or of baldness: that it is a mere question of words, to be settled by a stipulation. Yet these and the others are all equally questions within a manmade verbal fabric, connected only more or less remotely with observation—too remotely, in all four cases, to be decidable. In what way, then, are the questions of heaps and baldness matters of convention, and the others matters of fact? One way to bring out the contrast is in terms of our physical theory itself, in full acceptance of bivalence. Namely, the number of the blades of grass and the presence of a hydrogen atom are physically determined by the spatio-temporal distribution of microphysical states, unknown though it be. Where to draw the line between heaps and nonheaps, on the other hand, or between the bald and the thatched, is not determined by the distribution of microphysical states, known or unknown; it remains an open option.

On this score the demarcation of the table surface is on a par with the cases of heaps and baldness. But it differs from those cases in not lending itself to any stipulation, however arbitrary, that we can formulate; so it can scarcely be called conventional. It is neither a matter of convention nor a matter of inscrutable but objective fact. Yet we are committed, nevertheless, to treating the table as one and not another of this multitude of imperceptibly divergent physical objects. Such is bivalence.

At this point one might defend bivalence by arguing that no actual sentence can hinge for its truth or falsity on demarcations of a table surface that are too subtle for us to formulate. But I find this defense unsatisfying. It is in the spirit of bivalence not just to treat each closed sentence as true or false; as Frege stressed, each general term must be definitely true or false of each object, specifiable or not. If the term 'table' is to be reconciled with bivalence, we must posit an exact demarcation, exact to the last molecule, even though we cannot specify it. We must hold that there are physical objects, coincident except for one molecule, such that one is a table and the other is not.

One might then despair of bivalence and proceed disconsolately to survey its fuzzy and plurivalent alternatives in hopes of finding something viable, however unlovely. Or one might dig in one's heels—recalcitrate, in a word—and accept this démarche as a lesson rather in the scope and limits of the notion of linguistic convention.

Bivalence is a basic trait of our classical theories of nature. It has us positing a true-false dichotomy across all the statements that we can express in our theoretical vocabulary, irrespective of our knowing how to decide them. In keeping with our theories of nature we have viewed all such sentences as having factual content, however remote from observation. In this way simplicity of theory has been served. What we now observe is that bivalence requires us further to view each general term, for example 'table', as true or false of objects even in the absence of what we in our bivalent way are prepared to recognize as objective fact. At this point, if not before, the creative element in theory-building may be felt to be getting out of hand, and second thoughts on bivalence may arise.

It may still be noted in mitigation that the notion of physical object in the liberal sense involves no such quandary, covering as it does indiscriminately all the competing candidates for the title of table. It and other notions of austere physical theory remain in the clear. It is only the common-sense classifications of physical objects that come into question.

4

✄ On the Very Idea of a Third Dogma

Truth, meaning, and belief are sticky concepts. They stick together. That meaning and truth were somehow closely related was evident before Russell's eponymous *Inquiry* and after, but it was left to Davidson to recognize Tarski's theory of truth as the very structure of a theory of meaning. This insight was a major advance in semantics. Tarski had indeed called his theory of truth a study in semantics, but one felt constrained to add that it was semantics only in a broad sense, belonging more specifically to the theory of reference and not to the theory of meaning. That constraint now lapses.

The pairing of meaning and belief is another point stressed by Davidson. They can be separated, like Siamese twins, only by artificial means. If we try to construe an unknown language, we may assume at best that the observed utterance describes the given situation as the speaker, not we, believes it to be. What we take the utterance to mean will then hinge on what we take the speaker to believe and vice versa. The utterance and the situation are the end points of a diagonal whose resolution into rectangular components, meaning and belief, depends on how we tilt the grid.

But it is the remaining pair, truth and belief, that seems to me to have got unobservedly stuck. I shall argue that it is because of conflating these at a crucial point that Davidson abandons what he calls the third dogma, thereby parting the last mooring of empiricism. He writes that "this . . .

dualism of scheme and content, of organizing system and something waiting to be organized, cannot be made intelligible and defensible. It is itself a dogma of empiricism, a third dogma. The third, and perhaps the last, for if we give it up it is not clear that there is anything distinctive left to call empiricism."[1] Against this purported dogma he argues that "the notion of fitting the totality of experience, like the notion of fitting the facts, or being true to the facts, adds nothing intelligible to the simple concept of being true . . . Nothing, . . . no *thing*, makes sentences and theories true: not experience, not surface irritations, not the world."[2]

He rightly protests in these pages and elsewhere that it is idle to say that true sentences are sentences that fit the facts, or match the world; also pernicious, in creating an illusion of explanation. There is nothing to add to Tarski's analysis, Davidson rightly urges, so far as the concept of truth is concerned. Where I sense a conflation of truth and belief, however, is in his referring to "the totality of experience" and "surface irritations" on a par with "the facts" and "the world." The proper role of experience or surface irritation is as a basis not for truth but for warranted belief.

If empiricism is construed as a theory of truth, then what Davidson imputes to it as a third dogma is rightly imputed and rightly renounced. Empiricism as a theory of truth thereupon goes by the board, and good riddance. As a theory of evidence, however, empiricism remains with us, minus indeed the two old dogmas. The third purported dogma, understood now in relation not to truth but to warranted belief, remains intact. It has both a descriptive and a normative aspect, and in neither aspect do I think of it as a dogma. It is what makes scientific method partly empirical rather than solely a quest for internal coherence. It has indeed wanted some tidying up, and has had it.

The last section of my "Two Dogmas of Empiricism"[3] is cited by many writers in varied moods, and Davidson has not spared it. It is where I represented total science as "a

---

1. "On the very idea of a conceptual scheme," p. 11.
2. *Ibid.*, p. 16.
3. Reprinted in *From a Logical Point of View*.

man-made fabric which impinges on experience only along
the edges. Or, to change the figure, . . . a field of force whose
boundary conditions are experience." It was an interim in-
dication of an attitude, and an attitude that I still hold. My
noncommittal term 'experience' awaited a theory.

Within four years I was referring more committally to
surface irritations. I took this line so as to discourage a
phenomenalistic interpretation. Our typical sentences are
about bodies and substances, assumed or known in varying
degrees, out in the world. Typically they are not about sense
data or experiences or, certainly, surface irritations. But
some of them are elicited by surface irritations, and others
are related to surface irritations in less direct and more
tenuous ways.

If there was still an unintended overtone of sensory
quality in my reference to surface irritation, it was effectively banished by the time I wrote *Word and Object;* for
there I wrote explicitly of the triggering of sensory receptors. Nobody could suppose that I supposed that people are
on the whole thinking or talking about the triggering of
their nerve endings; few people, statistically speaking, know
about their nerve endings.

Putting matters thus physiologically was of a piece with
my naturalism, my rejection of a first philosophy underlying science. Empiricist discipline, however, is not lost
thereby. The fabric celebrated in my old metaphor is with
us still. As before it is a fabric of sentences accepted in
science as true, however provisionally. The ones at the edges
are occasion sentences. Moreover, they are occasion sentences of a special sort, namely, ones whose acceptance as
true on any given occasion is apt to be prompted by the firing
of associated sets or patterns of receptors on that occasion.
The tribunal, to worry another of my old metaphors, is just
the firing of the receptors.

I assume no awareness of the firing or any interim con-
templation of sense data. I treat of stimulus and response.
The response is assertion of the occasion sentence or assent
to it. Typically the sentence is one that treats of external
objects and is not devoid of theoretical terms. The link be-

tween the stimulus and the response is forged in some cases by simple conditioning or ostension and in other cases by analogy or verbal explanation, but it becomes a direct and immediate connection once it is forged.

Where empiricist discipline persists is partly in the relative firmness of this link between a goodly store of occasion sentences and concurrent stimulation, and partly in a high degree of dependence upon these occasion sentences on the part of sentences in the interior of the fabric. It is a matter of degree of responsivness, a matter of more and less responsible science, of better and worse.

It seems that in Davidson's mind the purported third dogma is somehow bound up with a puzzling use on my part of the phrase "conceptual scheme." The "dualism of scheme and content" deplored in my first quotation from Davidson bears a trace of this, as does the title of his essay. In conclusion, then, let me clarify the status of the phrase. I inherited it some forty-five years ago through L. J. Henderson from Pareto, and I have meant it as ordinary language, serving no technical function. It is not, as architects say, a supporting member. A triad—conceptual scheme, language, and world—is not what I envisage. I think rather, like Davidson, in terms of language and the world. I scout the *tertium quid* as a myth of a museum of labeled ideas. Where I have spoken of a conceptual scheme I could have spoken of a language. Where I have spoken of a very alien conceptual scheme I would have been content, Davidson will be glad to know, to speak of a language awkward or baffling to translate.

Somewhere I suggested a measure of what might be called the remoteness of a conceptual scheme but what might better be called the conceptual distance between languages. The definition hinges on changes in the lengths of sentences under translation. Given a pair of sentences from the two languages, sentences that are acceptable translations of each other, select a shortest equivalent of each of the sentences within its language. Compare these two shortest equivalents in respect of length, and compute the ratio. When this has been done for every pair of sentences that are acceptable translations of each other, strike the average of all those ratios. This measures the conceptual distance between the two languages.

Sentences are infinitely numerous, for want of a limit on length, and so therefore are pairs of sentences. The striking of that average ratio is consequently no simple matter of division; we must consider limits of infinite series. There is also the indeterminacy of translation to contend with, but we can accommodate that by so choosing our manual of translation, from among the multitude of empirically correct ones, as to minimize that average ratio of lengths of sentences that we are angling for.

What I have offered is not, I hardly need say, an effective procedure. But it does afford a definition of a sort, and one that is not much vaguer than the notion of acceptable translation on which it depends.

The vagueness of the notion of acceptable translation is not, indeed, a vagueness to belittle. If there is a question in my mind whether a language might be so remote as to be largely untranslatable, and hence beyond the reach even of the definition of remoteness that I have simulated above, that question arises from the vagueness of the very notion of translation. We are already accustomed, after all, to cutting corners and tolerating rough approximations even in neighborly translation. Translatability is a flimsy notion, unfit to bear the weight of the theories of cultural incommensurability that Davidson effectively and justly criticizes.

5

Use and Its Place
in Meaning

Words and phrases refer to things in either of two ways. A name or singular description *designates* its object, if any. A predicate *denotes* each of the objects of which it is true. Such are the two sorts of reference: designation and denotation. We are often told, and rightly, that neither sort is to be confused with *meaning*. The descriptions 'the author of *Waverley*' and 'the author of *Ivanhoe*' designate the same man, after all, but differ in meaning; and a predicate may denote each of many things while having only one meaning.

There are no restraints on what can be referred to. All sorts of things are designated and denoted. On the other hand, a meaning is apparently some special sort of thing. But just what?

You would think we would know. The word 'meaning' is a common noun, a very common noun, on the tip of everyone's tongue. It occurs in a few frequent phrases. We ask the

The opening pages of this essay were those of "Cognitive meaning" *The Monist*, vol. 62:2, April 1979, and are reprinted with the permission of the editor and the publisher. The rest was presented under the present title in a symposium on meaning and use that was held in Jerusalem in April 1976 in memory of Bar-Hillel. It appeared in the symposium volume *Meaning and Use* (Avishai Margalit, ed., copyright © 1979, D. Reidel Publishing Co., Dordrecht, Holland), pp. 1–8, and meanwhile in *Erkenntnis* 13 (copyright © 1978, D. Reidel), likewise pp. 1–8.

meaning of a word; we give the meaning of a word; we speak of knowing the meaning of an expression; we speak of an expression as having or lacking meaning; and we speak of expressions as alike in meaning. But one context in which we do not normally encounter the word 'meaning' is the context 'a meaning is'; 'a meaning *is* such and such'. The question. 'What is a meaning?' thus qualifies as a peculiarly philosophical question.

Meanings are meanings of expressions, so I had better begin by explaining my use of the expression 'expression'. An expression, for me, is a string of phonemes—or, if we prefer to think in terms of writing, a string of letters and spaces. Some expressions are sentences. Some are words. Thus when I speak of a sentence, or of a word, I am again referring to the sheer string of phonemes and nothing more. I must stress this because there is a widespread usage to the contrary. The word or sentence is often thought of rather as a combination, somehow, of a string of phonemes and a meaning. Homonyms are thus treated as distinct words. This usage is often convenient in the study of language, and in its proper place I have no quarrel with it. But it cannot be allowed here, because our purpose is to isolate and clarify the notion of meaning.

A meaning, still, is something that an expression, a string of phonemes, may *have,* as something external to it in the way in which a man may have an uncle or a bank account. It has it by virtue of how the string of phonemes is used by people. The same expression, the same string, may by coincidence turn up in two languages and mean differently in them. It may mean in two ways even in a single language; and then it is called ambiguous. But it remains, in any sense, one and the same expression. On this approach ambiguity and homonymy are on a par: what is concerned in either case is a single string of phonemes.

The point is that the notion of an expression must not be allowed to presuppose the notion of meaning. One may suspect, however, that my identifying expressions with strings of phonemes is then self-defeating, because the notion of a phoneme is itself commonly so defined as to presuppose the notion of sameness and difference of meaning. Two

acoustically distinguishable sounds are counted as occurrences of the same phoneme if substitution of the one sound
for the other leaves meanings unaffected. Now this appeal
to meaning is happily not needed. We can simply say that two
sounds count as occurrences of the same phoneme if the substitution has no effect on a speaker's readiness to assent to
any string of sounds.

Expressions, then, are strings of phonemes in this innocent sense, and it is expressions that are to have meanings. What sort of things these meanings are is the question
before us. But actually we are rather rushing matters in supposing there to be such things as meanings; for one can perhaps talk of meaning without talking of meanings.

Thus let us start rather with the verb 'mean' as an intransitive verb. An expression means; meaning is what it
does, or what some expressions do. To say that two expressions are alike in meaning, then, is to say that they mean
alike. Some expressions sound alike, some mean alike. It is
significant that when we ask for the meaning of an expression we are content to be given another expression on a par
with the first—like it in meaning. We do not ask for something that the two of them mean. The French idiom is more
to the point: *cela veut dire.*

We could wish for further light on just what an expression is doing when it means, and how it does it, but we need
not seek anything that the expression is doing it to—any-
things that gets meant. We are not tempted to if we take
'mean' as intransitive.

In a longer view, however, this bid for ontological econ-
omy is idle. For, once we understand what it is for expressions to mean alike, it is easy and convenient to invoke some
special objects arbitrarily and *let* them be meant—thus re-
constituting our verb as transitive. In choosing a domain of
objects for this purpose and assigning them to expressions
as their so-called meanings, all that matters is that the same
one be assigned always and only to expressions that mean
alike. If we can manage this, then we can blithely say thereafter that expressions that mean alike *have* the *same meaning*. We should merely bear in mind that 'mean alike' comes
first, and the so-called meanings are then concocted.

How do we concoct them? I said it was easy. Just take
each meaning as a set of expressions that mean alike. The
meaning of an expression is the set of all expressions that
mean like it. Clearly this definition, which is by no means
new, meets the stated requirement: it assigns the same
meaning to two expressions if and only if they mean alike.
The air of artificiality is no drawback, since there was no
preconception as to what sort of thing a meaning ought to be.

So we see that if we know what it is for expressions to
mean alike, the rest is easy. And we would seem to know, if
facile lip service were indicative; but it is not. Fluency and
clarity are poorly correlated.

Wittgenstein has stressed that the meaning of a word is
to be sought in its use. This is where the empirical semanti-
cist looks: to verbal behavior. John Dewey was urging this
point in 1925. "Meaning," he wrote (p. 179), ". . . is primarily a property of behavior." And just what property of behavior might meaning then be? Well, we can take the behavior, the use, and let the meaning go.

How, then, may we set about studying the use of words?
Take a decidedly commonplace and unambiguous word:
'desk'. What are the circumstances of my use of this word?
They include, perhaps, all the sentences in which I ever have
used or shall use the word, and all the stimulatory situations
in which I uttered or shall utter those sentences. Perhaps
they include all the sentences and stimulatory situations in
which I *would* use the word. The sentences and stimulatory
situations in which I *would now* use the word might even
be said to constitute the *meaning* of the word for me now,
if we care to rehabilitate the dubious term 'meaning'. However, the range of sentences and stimulatory situations concerned is forbiddingly vast and ill organized. Where is one
to begin?

For a provisional solution, consider what we often actually do when asked the meaning of a word: we define the
word by equating it to some more familiar word or phrase.
Now this is itself a quick way of specifying the range of sentences and situations in which the word is used. We are
specifying that range by identifying it with the range of sentences and stimulations in which the other and more familiar

word or phrase is used. Happily we can spare ourselves the trouble of cataloguing all those sentences and situations, because our pupil has already mastered the use of the more familiar word or phrase.

We may persist, then, in the old routine of giving meanings by citing synonyms. The behavioral doctrine of meaning does not oppose that. What the behavioral doctrine of meaning contributes is theoretical: it purports to explain this synonymy relation itself, the relation between the word whose meaning is asked and the more familiar word or phrase that we cite in reply. The behavioral doctrine tells us that this relation of synonymy, or sameness of meaning, is sameness of use.

The method of giving the meaning of a word by citing a synonym is convenient but very limited. It accounts for only a small minority of the entries in a dictionary. Often the lexicographer will resort to what he calls a distinction of senses: he will cite several partial synonyms, some suitable in some kinds of context and others in others. When he does this, he has to distinguish the kinds of context by providing a general characterization of each, usually by reference to subject matter. And in many cases there is no such appeal even to partial synonyms; the use of a word can be taught in other ways. In general, given any sentence all of whose words are familiar except the word in question, what needs to be taught is how to paraphrase that sentence into an equivalent whose words are all familiar.

General instructions for paraphrasing the sentential contexts of a word into unproblematic sentences: such is the lexicographer's job. The citing of a direct synonym is just one form that such instructions may take, and it is feasible less often than not. What is more to the point than the relation of synonymy of words to words and phrases, then, as a central concept for semantics, is the relation of semantical equivalence of whole sentences. Given this concept, we readily define the other: a word is synonymous to a word or phrase if the substitution of the one for the other in a sentence always yields an equivalent sentence.

And when do sentences count as semantically equivalent? A provisional answer from the behavior point of view is evident: they are equivalent if their use is the same. Or, trying to put the matter less vaguely, we might say that they are equivalent if their utterance would be prompted by the same stimulatory situations.

But clearly this will not do. They cannot both be uttered at once; one must be uttered to the exclusion of the other. On any occasion where one of the sentences is uttered, moreover, there must have been a cause, however trivial, for uttering it rather than the other. It may hinge merely on a phonetic accident: the choice of a word in the one sentence may have been triggered by a chance phonetic resemblance to a word just previously heard. Clearly we ask too much if we ask of two equivalent sentences that they be prompted by all the same stimulations. And anyway, if a criterion required actually comparing the stimulatory conditions for the volunteering of sentences, it would surely be hopeless in practice; for utterances are on the whole virtually unpredictable. The motives for volunteering a given sentence can vary widely, and often inscrutably: the speaker may want to instruct, or console, or surprise, or amuse, or impress, or relieve a painful silence, or influence someone's behavior by deception.

We can cut through all this if we limit our attention to the *cognitive* equivalence of sentences; that is, to the sameness of truth conditions. We are then spared having to speculate on the motives or circumstances for volunteering a sentence. Instead we can arrange the circumstances ourselves and volunteer the sentence ourselves, in the form of a query, asking only for a verdict of true or false. Cognitively equivalent sentences will get matching verdicts, at least if we keep to the same speaker. He can be mistaken in his verdicts, but no matter; he will then make the same mistake on both sentences.

I remarked that it would be too much to require of two equivalent sentences that their utterance be prompted by all the same stimulations. Now, however, we are evidently in an opposite difficulty: we are requiring too little. We are requiring only that the speaker believe both or disbelieve both or suspend judgment on both. This way lies little more than material equivalence, not cognitive equivalence.

The solution to this difficulty is to be found in what John Stuart Mill called concomitant variation. To get this effect we must limit our attention for a while in yet another way: we must concentrate on occasion sentences. These, as opposed to standing sentences, are sentences whose truth values change from occasion to occasion, so that a fresh verdict has to be prompted each time. Typically they are sentences that contain indexical words, and that depend essentially on tenses of verbs. Examples are 'This is red' and 'There goes a rabbit'; these might be designated more particularly as observation sentences. Further examples are 'He is a bachelor' and 'There goes John's old tutor'; these do not qualify as observation sentences, but still they are occasion sentences. The truth value of 'He is a bachelor' varies with the reference of the pronoun from occasion to occasion; similarly the truth value of 'There goes John's old tutor' depends both on the varying reference of the name 'John' and on who happens to be passing down the street at the time. Now if our interrogated informant is disposed to give matching verdicts on two such occasion sentences on every occasion on which we query the two sentences, no matter what the attendant circumstances, then certainly the two sentences must be said to be cognitively equivalent for him. One such pair is 'He is a bachelor' and 'He is an unmarried man'. Another such pair, for a particular speaker, may be 'There goes John's old tutor' and 'There goes Dr. Park'.

These two pairs of examples differ significantly from each other, in that the second pair qualifies as cognitively equivalent only for a particular speaker, or a few speakers, while the first pair would qualify as cognitively equivalent for each speaker of the language. It is the difference between cognitive equivalence for an individual, or for an idiolect, and cognitive equivalence for a language. It is the latter that we are interested in when we expound the semantics of a language. Cognitive equivalence for the individual, however, is the prior notion conceptually, that is, in respect of criterion. Two occasion sentences are equivalent for him if he is disposed, on every occasion of query, to give them matching verdicts or, on doubtful occasions, no verdict.

The summation over society comes afterward: the sentences are equivalent for the language if equivalent for each speaker taken separately.

This unanimity requirement works all right for our core language, Basic English so to say, which all English speakers command. However, when recondite words are admitted, a pair of occasion sentences may fail of cognitive equivalence for an ignorant speaker merely because of misunderstanding. If we still want to count those two sentences cognitively equivalent for the language, we may do so by relativizing the unanimity requirement to an elite subset of the population.

Cognitive equivalence of two occasion sentences for a speaker consists in his being disposed to give matching verdicts when queried in matching stimulatory circumstances. We can easily make this notion of stimulatory circumstances more explicit. It is a question of the external forces that impinge on the interrogated subject at the time, and these only insofar as they affect his nervous system by triggering his sensory receptors. Thanks to the all-or-none law, there are no degrees or respects of triggering to distinguish. So, without any loss of relevant information, we may simply identify the subject's external stimulation at each moment with the set of his triggered receptors. Even this identification is very redundant, since the triggering of some receptors will have no effect on behavior, and the triggering of some receptors will have no different effect from what the triggering of other neighboring receptors would have had. However, the redundancy is harmless. Its effect is merely that two occasion sentences that are cognitively equivalent, in the sense of commanding like verdicts under identical stimulations, will also command like verdicts under somewhat unlike stimulations.

Each overall momentary stimulation of our interrogated subject is to be identified, I have suggested, with a subset of his receptors. The stimulation that he undergoes at any moment is the set of receptors triggered at that moment. This makes good sense of sameness and difference of stimulation of that person from moment to moment. It does not make sense of sameness of stimulation of two persons, since two persons do not share the same receptors. They do not even have exactly homologous receptors, if we get down to minutiae. But this is all very well, for I am not having to equate stimulations between persons. The notion of cognitive equivalence of occasion sentences for a single person rests on sameness and difference of stimulations of that person alone, and the subsequent summation over society appeals then to cognitive equivalence for each separate person, with no equating of stimulations between persons.

I feel that the relation of cognitive equivalence is in good shape, so far as occasion sentences are concerned. The relation is defined for the individual and for society, and the definition can be applied by a routine of query and verdict. There remain, of course, the other sentences—the standing sentences.

There remain also the single words, and their relation of synonymy to other words and phrases. We saw earlier that this relation presents no difficulty, once we have fixed the relation of equivalence of sentences. One word is synonymous to another word or phrase if substitution of the one for the other always yields equivalent sentences. Or, now that our equivalence relation for sentences is cognitive equivalence, we should say that a word is *cognitively* synonymous to a word or phrase if substitution of the one for the other always yield cognitively equivalent sentences. Granted, the relation even of cognitive equivalence of sentences is now under control only for occasion sentences. However, I think this is already enough to settle cognitive synonymy of words to words and phrases across the board. If a given word is interchangeable with a given word or phrase in all occasion sentences, invariably yielding a cognitively equivalent sentence, then I think the interchangeability can be depended on to hold good in all standing sentences as well.

If this be granted, then a conceptual foundation for cognitive synonymy is pretty firmly laid. The courses, as stonemasons call them, are as follows. First there is the relation of sameness of overall stimulation of an individual at different times. This is defined, theoretically, by sameness of triggered receptors. Next there is the relation of cognitive equivalence of occasion sentences for the individual. This is defined by his disposition to give matching verdicts when the two sentences are queried under identical overall stimulations. Next there is the relation of cognitive equivalence of occasion sentences for the whole linguistic community. This is defined as cognitive equivalence for each individual. Finally there is the relation of cognitive synonymy of a word to a word or phrase. This is defined as interchangeability in occasion sentences *salva aequalitate*. We could take the nominal further step, if we liked, and define the cognitive meaning of a word as the set of its cognitive synonyms.

Strictly speaking, this interchangeability criterion of synonymy requires some awkward reservations regarding the positions in which the substitutions are allowable. For instance, it would never do to require interchangeability within direct quotations; and this reservation extends, in diminishing degrees, to indirect quotation and other idioms of propositional attitude. I shall pass over this difficulty, for it is a familiar and perennial one, and I have nothing new to say about it.

Anyway we must remember that the synonymy of words and phrases, however well defined, is not the mainstay of lexicography. What are wanted in general, as I said earlier, are instructions for paraphrasing the sentential contexts of a word into unproblematic sentences by whatever means; the citing of a direct synonym is just one form that such instructions can sometimes take. The relation of equivalence of occasion sentences offers a foundation equally, however, for all this. If the use of a word can be pinned down by instructions for paraphrasing its sentential contexts at all, I expect it can be pinned down by instructions for paraphrasing just those contexts that are occasion sentences.

If we may measure the familiarity of words by their frequency, we may perhaps schematize the task of the monoglot lexicographer as follows. Let us define a *gloss* of a sentence s, with respect to one of its words w, as any cognitively equivalent sentence lacking w and containing only other words of s and words of higher frequency than w. A word may be called *reducible* if all occasion sentences that contain it admit of such glosses with respect to it. The lexicographer's task, then, is a systematic specification of glosses of occasion sentences with respect to all reducible words. This leaves him doing nothing about the irreducible words, which constitute the core language. I welcome this outcome on the whole, for the monoglot lexicographer's compulsive explanations of irreducible words have been a waste. But he should still add a few supplementary cognitive equivalences for the benefit of speakers whose frequencies diverge somewhat from the national average. For instance he should continue to define 'gorse' as 'furze' *and* 'furze' as 'gorse'.

I am of course stopping short still of the needs of practical lexicography in one conspicuous respect: I am attending only to the cognitive side, ignoring emotional and poetic aspects. Regarding those further aspects I have nothing to suggest.

My consideration of cognitive equivalence has been limited to occasion sentences thus far, and I have urged that occasion sentences already provide a broad enough base for lexicography. However, there is no need to limit cognitive equivalence to occasion sentences. We can extend the relation into standing sentences in several fragmentary but substantial ways. Standing sentences grade off into occasion sentences, after all. Verdicts on occasion sentences have to be prompted anew on each occasion, while verdicts on standing sentences may stand for various periods. The shorter the periods, the more the sentence resembles an occasion sentence. The more it resembles an occasion sentence, the more applicable our criterion of cognitive equivalence: the criterion of like verdicts under like stimulation. We might even extend this criterion to all standing sentences, provided that we take it only as a necessary condition of cognitive equivalence and not a sufficient one. For occasion sentences it is necessary and sufficient.

From another angle a sufficient but not necessary condition of cognitive equivalence can be brought to bear on standing sentences. Namely, we can exploit the relation of cognitive synonymy, which I already defined on the basis of cognitive equivalence of occasion sentences. One standing sentence is cognitively equivalent to another if it can be transformed into the other by a sequence of replacements of words or phrases by cognitive synonyms. This sufficient condition can be broadened by submitting the standing sentences not just

to substitution of synonyms but also to other sort of paraphrase: sorts that have already been found to preserve cognitive equivalence among occasion sentences.

These conditions do not quite add up to a definition of
cognitive equivalence for standing sentences. If a pair of
standing sentences meets the necessary condition and not
the proposed sufficient one, the question of their cognitive
equivalence has no answer. But in their incomplete way the
conditions do make the notion widely applicable to standing
sentences. Meanwhile it is defined for occasion sentences,
and this, I have urged, is basis enough for cognitive lexicography.

I have been concerned in all these remarks with monoglot
semantics, not polyglot; not translation. Criteria are harder
to come by in the polyglot domain, particularly in the case
of radical translation, where there are no bilinguals to exploit. The most serious difference is this: cognitive equivalence for a single individual is definable for occasion sentences generally, by sameness of verdict under sameness of
stimulation; but between two individuals this definition carries us little beyond the observation sentences.[1]

If a bilingual is available, we can treat the two languages
as his single tandem language; and then we can indeed define cognitive equivalence of occasion sentences generally,
for him, even between the languages. But this is still cognitive equivalence only for him and not for a linguistic community, or pair of communities. Only if we have a whole
subcommunity of bilinguals can we summate over the individuals, as we did in the monoglot case, and derive a bilingual relation of cognitive equivalence of occasion sentences at the social level. The polyglot case thrives, it would
seem, just to the extent that it can be treated as monoglot.
Thus the theory I have been developing here has no bear-
ing, that I can see, on the indeterminacy of translation.

1. See my *Word and Object*, pp. 41–49.

6

On the Nature of Moral Values

Imagine a dog idling in the foreground, a tree in the middle distance, and a turnip lying on the ground behind the tree. Either of two hypotheses, or a combination of them, may be advanced to explain the dog's inaction with respect to the turnip: perhaps he is not aware that it is there, and perhaps he does not want a turnip. Such is the bipartite nature of motivation: belief and valuation intertwined. It is the deep old duality of thought and feeling, of the head and the heart, the cortex and the thalamus, the words and the music.

The duality can be traced back to the simplest conditioning of responses. A response was rewarded when it followed stimulus a, and penalized when it followed b; and thereafter it tended to be elicited by just those stimulations that were more similar to a than to b according to the subject's inarticulate standards of similarity. Observe then the duality of belief and valuation: the similarity standards are the epistemic component of habit formation, in its primordial form, and the reward-penalty axis is the valuative component.

The term 'belief' of course ill fits this primitive level. Even the term 'similarity standard' requires a word of caution:

This essay was written for A. I. Goldman and J. Kim, eds., *Values and Morals* (copyright © 1978, D. Reidel Publishing Co., Dordrecht, Holland, pp. 37–46), a volume in honor of Brandt, Frankena, and Stevenson. It was reprinted in *Critical Inquiry* 5 (1979).

such implicit standards of similarity are ascribed to the subject only on the behavioral basis of the experiments themselves, experiments in the reinforcement and extinction of his responses. The experiments afford at the same time a criterion for comparing the subject's implicit values, along the reward-penalty axis. His values are easier to plot, however, than his similarities. They are largely recognizable from innate reflexes, such as wincing, even without recourse to experiments in reinforcement and extinction. Moreover, they stand in the simple dyadic relation of better and worse, whereas similarity is at least triadic: *a* is more similar to *b* than to *c*. The evaluations thus line up in a single dimension, while the similarities may be expected to require more dimensions.

Clearly all learning, all acquisition of dispositions to discriminatory behavior, requires in the subject this bipartite equipment: it requires a similarity space and it requires some ordering of episodes along the valuation axis, however crude. Some such equipment, then, must precede all learning; that is, it must be innate. There need be no question here of awareness, or of ideas, innate or otherwise. It is a matter rather of physiological details of our complex and incontestably innate nervous system, which determine our susceptibilities to the reinforcement and extinction of responses. Those details are perhaps not yet fully understood, but we need know little to be assured that what is required for all learning must not have been learned.

Our innate similarity space is our modest head start on the epistemic side, for it is the starting point for induction. Induction consists, primitively, in the expectation that similar episodes will have similar sequels; and the similarity concerned is similarity by our subjective lights. In our innate likes and dislikes we have our modest head start on the valuative side, and then induction is our guide to worthwhile acts. I find it instructive to dignify the lowly neural phenomenon of reinforcement and extinction in these subjectivist terms, for its represents that neural phenomenon as technology in the small: the use of inductive science for realizing values.

Our similarity space is progressively changed and elaborated as our learning proceeds. Similarity standards that led to bad predictions get readjusted by trial and error. Our inductions become increasingly explicit and deliberate, and in the fullness of time we even rise above induction, to the hypothetico-deductive method.

Likewise our ordering of sensory episodes along the valuation axis is progressively changed and elaborated. In some cases an epistemic factor contributes to the change. We learn by induction that one sort of event tends to lead to another that we prize, and then by a process of transfer we may come to prize the former not only as a means but for itself. We come to relish the sport of fishing as much as we relish the fresh trout to which it was a means. Values get shifted also in other ways—perhaps something to do with chemistry, in the case of the acquired taste for strong peppers or anchovies. Or in more baffling ways, if one moves on to Schönberg or Jackson Pollock.

The transmutation of means into ends, just now illustrated by fishing, is what underlies moral training. Many sorts of good behavior have a low initial rating on the valuation scale, and are indulged in at first only for their inductive links to higher ends: to pleasant consequences or the avoidance of unpleasant ones at the preceptor's hands. Good behavior, insofar, is technology. But by association of means with ends we come gradually to accord this behavior a higher intrinsic rating. We find satisfaction in engaging in it and we come to encourage it in others. Our moral training has succeeded. There are exceptions to this pattern of development, I regret to say, but happily not among my readers.

The penalties and rewards by which the good behavior was inculcated may have included slaps and sugar plums. However, mere show of approval and disapproval on the parent's part will go a long way. It seems that such bland manifestations can directly induce pleasure and discomfort already in the very young. Perhaps some original source of sensual satisfaction, such as a caress, comes to be associated very early with the other more subtle signs of parental approval, which then come to be prized in themselves.

The distinction between moral values and others is not an easy one. There are easy extremes: the value that one places on his neighbor's welfare is moral, and the value of peanut brittle is not. The value of decency in speech and dress is moral or ethical in the etymological sense, resting as it does on social custom; and similarly for observance of the Jewish dietary laws. On the other hand, the eschewing of unrefrigerated oysters in the summer, though it is likewise a renunciation of immediate fleshly pleasure, is a case rather of prudence than of morality. But presumably the Jewish taboos themselves began prudentially. Again a Christian fundamentalist who observes the proprieties and helps his neighbors only from fear of hell-fire is manifesting prudence rather than moral values.[1] Similarly for the man with felony in his heart who behaves himself for fear of the law. Similarly for the child who behaves himself in the course of moral training; his behavior counts as moral only after these means get transmuted into ends. On the other hand, the value that the child attaches to the parent's approval is a moral value. It had been a mere harbinger of a sensually gratifying caress, if my recent suggestion is right, but has been transmuted into an end in itself.

It is hard to pick out a single distinguishing feature of moral values, beyond the vague matter of being somehow irreducibly social. We do better to recognize two largely overlapping classes of moral values. *Altruistic* values are values that one attaches to satisfactions of other persons, or to means to such satisfactions, without regard to ulterior satisfactions accruing to oneself. *Ceremonial* values, as we might say, are values that one attaches to practices of one's society or social group, again without regard to ulterior satisfactions accruing to oneself. Definitions appealing explicitly to behavioral dispositions rather than thus to hidden motivations would be desirable, but meanwhile a vague sketch such as this can be of some help if we do not overestimate it.

It is clear from the foregoing examples of prudential taboos, hell-fire, repressed felony, and child training, that two members of a society may value an act equally and yet the

1. Bernard Williams, pp. 75f, questions the disjointness of these alternatives. I am construing them disjointly.

value may be moral for the one and prudential for the other. But we like to speak also of the moral values or moral code or morality of a society as a whole. In so doing we may perhaps be taken to mean those values that are implemented by social sanctions, plus any further values that are moral values for most of the members individually.

I follow Schlick in placing the moral values in among the sensual and aesthetic values on an equal footing. Some non-moral values, for instance that of fishing, are subject to transmutation of means into ends, and some are innate, and some accrue in other ways. But so it is in particular with moral values: some accrue by transmutation of means into ends, through training, and some perhaps require no training.

Schlick, like Hume, set great store by sympathy: by the pleasure and sorrow that are induced by witnessing others' pleasure and sorrow. We have these susceptibilities, he believed, without training. If they are somehow gene-linked, it would be interesting to understand the mechanism. This would then account also for the previous point, the infant's early responsiveness to signs of parental approval and disapproval, as a special case.

Tinbergen in his study of herring gulls determined what simple configurations on paper served to rouse the chick to an expectant attitude, as if toward its mother, and what configurations would arouse a complementary attitude in the hen. He noted a human analogue in the simple formula for 'cuteness': fat cheek, big eye, negligible nose. Disney knew how to induce audible female cooing in the movie theater with a few strokes of the pen. The herring gull's response is instinctive; must ours, in this case, be otherwise? Again the rabbit that squeals from between the wolf's jaws is making an instinctive response that is altruistic in a functional sense; for the squeal does not deter the wolf, but it warns other rabbits. Hereditary altruism at its heroic extreme raises a genetic question, if the young martyr is not to live to transmit his altruistic genes; but biologists have proposed an answer. Altruism is mainly directed to close kin, and they transmit largely the same genes.

I represented our moral values as falling into two overlapping classes, the altruistic and the ceremonial. The classes overlap in two ways. Altruistic values are in part institutionalized and so may take on an added ceremonial appeal. Conversely, there is altruistic value in so behaving as not to offend against a neighbor's ceremonial values.

There are also cross-classifications, imposed by considerations of origin. Some values, in the altruistic category, perhaps issue freely from an innate faculty of sympathy, unless this class is empty and sympathy is an acquired taste. Some, in the ceremonial category, are embraced out of sentiments of solidarity; thus the dietary observances in some cases, and the old school tie. The basis here is perhaps sympathy still, in an attenuated way. Further, in any event, there are both altruistic and ceremonial values that are inculcated by precept, unsupported still by palpable reward or punishment. This is already a case of training in its mild way, a case of transmutation of means into ends; the good behavior is indulged in at first as a means to the ethereal end of parental or social approval, and only afterward comes to be valued as an end in itself. Finally, there is moral training by recourse to palpable reward or punishment over and above parental or social attitude. Few of us are of such saintly docility as to need no training of this earthier kind. But in due course, here again, means get transmuted into ends, and conscience is further fortified.

I remarked that this account places the moral values in among the sensual and aesthetic ones. By the same token it represents each of us as pursuing exclusively his own private satisfactions. Thanks to the moral values that have been trained into us, however, plus any innate moral beginnings that there may have been, there is no clash of interests as we pursue our separate ways. Our scales of values blend in social harmony.

I am using the first-person plural rather narrowly here, to include my readers and myself but not as many further persons as I could wish. There are those—I mention no names—whose moral training has been neglected or has not proved feasible. Their ordering of values has remained in such a state that these persons stand to maximize their satisfactions by battening on our good behavior while cheating on their own. Society accommodates such misfits by introducing penalties to offset the imbalance in their values.

The moral values tend by virtue of their social character to be more uniform from person to person, within a culture, than many sensual and aesthetic values. Hence the tendency with regard to the latter to allow that *de gustibus non disputandum est,* while ascribing absoluteness and even divine origin to the moral law.

Hypotheses less extravagant than that of divine origin account well enough for such uniformity as obtains among moral values, even apart from possible innate components. It is merely that these values are passed down the generations, imposed by word of mouth, by birch rod and sugar plum, by acclaim and ostracism, fine, imprisonment. They are imposed by society because they matter to society, whereas aesthetic preferences may be left to go their way.

Language, like the moral law, was once thought to be God-given. The two have much in common. Both are institutions for the common good. Taken together they reflect, somewhat, the primitive duality of belief and valuation on which I remarked at the beginning. Language promotes the individual's inductions by giving him access to his neighbor's observations and even to his neighbor's finished inductions. It also helps him influence his neighbor's actions, but it does this mainly, still, by conveying factual information. On the other hand, the moral law of a society, if successful, coordinates the actual scales of values of the individuals in such a way as to resolve incompatibilities and thus promote their overall satisfaction.

In language there is a premium on uniformity of usage, to facilitate communication. In morality there is a premium on uniformity of moral values, so that we may count on one another's actions and rise in a body against a transgressor. In language as in morality the uniformity is achieved by instruction, each generation teaching the next. In the case of language there is less recourse to birch rod and sugar plum, because the rewards of conformity are built in. In morals, private deviations such as theft can augment one's satisfactions unless one's values have been rearranged by moral training or offset by external sanctions; but in language, private deviation directly defeats one's own immediate purpose by obscuring one's message. There is, however, an exception: lying is a deviation in verbal behavior that can work to one's private advantage. The utility of language for each of us hinges on a predominance of truthfulness on the part of others, but any of us can enjoy that advantage and lie a little too, to his private profit. Thus it is that the liar invites the reproaches not of the orthoepist but of the moralist. Moral values need to be instilled into him that will offset the values served by lying. Failing that, we may incapacitate his future lies by spreading warnings.

For the usefulness of a language it is required that most speakers associate the same expression with the same sort of object, but it does not matter how the expression sounds as long as all members of the society make it sound about alike. An expression to the same purpose in another language can therefore differ utterly and it will not matter, if the two societies do not seek to communicate. Language thus tends to extreme uniformity within isolated societies and chaotic diversity between them. We see linguistic gradation in the world, but only because of gradations in the intimacy of communication.

Moral values may be expected to vary less radically than language from one society to another, even when the societies are isolated. True, there are societies whose bans and licenses boggle our sheltered imaginations. But we can expect a common core, since the most basic problems of societies are bound to run to type. Morality touches the common lot of mankind as the particularities of sound and syntax do not. Where language touches the common lot is rather in the intelligence and influence that the sounds and syntax serve to convey. Thus any variation of morality from culture to culture invites comparison perhaps with the variation of world view or scientific outlook from culture to culture, but certainly not with the extravagant variation of language.

When we set about comparing moralities from culture to culture, assessing variations and seeking the common core, we may begin by considering how to separate the native's moral values from his other values. How much of what he does or refrains from doing is attributable to mistaken notions of causal efficacy on his part, and accountable therefore to misguided prudence rather than to moral scruples? He may believe in so full a complement of supernatural sanctions as to leave no scope for moral values as distinct from prudential ones. In this event we can do no better than recur to our derivative concept of the morality of a society, as distinct from that of an individual. The question then becomes that of determining what behavior is implemented by socially established rewards and penalties. This standard will fail us too, however, if the society is so successfully indoctrinated regarding supernatural sanctions that no social enforcement is called for. At this point the most we can do is compare the native's acts with ours in situations where our qualify as moral acts by our own lights. We will observe whether he respects property, and, if he does not, whether he seems worried and furtive in taking it. We will observe whether he kills harmless creatures without meaning to eat them. We will try to observe whether he is promiscuous in his love life, and, if so, whether he is furtive about that. We can observe his behavior, when he lets us, and we can applaud or reprehend it in our way.

Moral contrasts are not, of course, so far to seek. Disagreements on moral matters can arise at home, and even within oneself. When they do, one regrets the methodological infirmity of ethics as compared with science. The empirical foothold of scientific theory is in the predicted observable event; that of a moral code is in the observable moral act. But whereas we can test a prediction against the independent course of observable nature, we can judge the morality of an act only by our moral standards themselves. Science, thanks to its links with observation, retains some title to a correspondence theory of truth; but a coherence theory is evidently the lot of ethics.

Scientific theories on all sorts of useful and useless topics are sustained by empirical controls, partial and devious though they be. It is a bitter irony that so vital a matter as the difference between good and evil should have no comparable claim to objectivity. No wonder there have been efforts since earliest times to work a justification of moral values into the fabric of what might pass for factual science.

For such, surely, were the myths of divine origins of moral law.

There is a legitimate mixture of ethics with science that somewhat mitigates the methodological predicament of ethics. Anyone who is involved in moral issues relies on causal connections. Ethical axioms can be minimized by reducing some values causally to others; that is, by showing that some of the valued acts would already count as valuable anyway as means to ulterior ends. Utilitarianism is a notable example of such systematization.

Causal reduction can serve not only in thus condensing the assumptions but also in sorting out conflicts. Thus take the question of white lies. If we once agree to regard truthfulness as good only as a means to higher moral ends, rather than as an ultimate end in itself, then the question becomes a question essentially of science, or engineering. On the one hand, the utility of language requires a preponderance of truthfulness; on the other hand, the truth can cause pain. So one may try to puzzle out a strategy.

Causal reduction is often effective in resolving moral conflicts not only within the individual but between individuals. One individual disputes another's position on some point of morals. The other individual tries to justify his position instrumentally, hence by causal reduction to some ulterior end which they both value. The first individual is then either persuaded or proceeds to contest the causal reduction, in which case the issue has been gratefully transformed into a cognitive question of science. This way of resolving moral issues is successful to the extent that we can reduce moral values causally to other moral values that command agreement. There must remain some ultimate ends, unreduced and so unjustified. Happily these, once identified, would tend to be widely accepted. For we may expect a tendency to uniformity in the hereditary component of morality, whatever it may be, and also, since the basic problems of societies are much alike, we may expect considerable agreement in the socially imposed component when it is reduced to fundamentals.

Even in the extreme case where disagreement extends irreducibly to ultimate moral ends, the proper counsel is not one of pluralistic tolerance. One's disapproval of gratuitous torture, for example, easily withstands one's failure to make a causal reduction, and so be it. We can still call the good good and the bad bad, and hope with Stevenson that these epithets may work their emotive weal. In an extremity we can fight, if the threat to the ultimate value in question outweighs the disvalue of the fighting.

There remains the awkward matter of a conflict of ultimate values within the individual. It could have to do with the choice of a career, or mate, or vacation spot. The predicament in such a nonmoral case will concern only the individual and a few associates. When the ultimate values concerned are moral ones, on the other hand, and more particularly altruistic ones, the case is different; for the individual in such a dilemma has all society on his conscience.

The basic difficulty is that the altruistic values that we acquire by social conditioning and perhaps by heredity are vague and open-ended. Primitively the premium is on kin, and primitively therefore the very boundary of the tribe itself in its isolation constitutes a bold boundary between the beneficiaries of one's altruism and the alien world. Nowadays the boundary has given way to gradations. Moreover, we are prone to extrapolate; extrapolation was always intrinsic to induction, that primitive propensity that is at the root of all science. Extrapolation in science, however, is under the welcome restraint of stubborn fact: failures of prediction. Extrapolation in morals has only our unsettled moral values themselves to answer to, and it is these that the extrapolation was meant to settle.

Today we unhesitatingly extrapolate our altruism beyond our close community. Most of us extend it to all mankind. But to what degree? One cannot reasonably be called upon to love even one's neighbor *quite* as oneself. Is love to diminish inversely as the square of the distance? Is it to extend, in some degree, to the interests of individuals belonging to other species than our own? As regards capricious killing, one hopes so; but what of vivisection, and of the eating of red meat?

One thinks also of unborn generations. Insofar as our moral standards were shaped by evolution for fostering the

survival of the race, a concern for the unborn was assured.
One then proceeds, however, as one will, to systematize and
minimize one's ethical axioms by reducing some causally to
others. This effort at system-building leads to the formulation and scrutiny of principles, and one is then taken aback
by the seeming absurdity of respecting the interests of non-
existent people: of unactualized possibilities. This counter-
revolutionary bit of moral rationalization is welcome as it
touches population control, since the blind drive to mass
procreation is now so counter-productive. But the gratification is short-lived, for the same rationalization would seem
to condone a despoiling of the environment for the exclusive
convenience of people now living.

It need not. A formulation is ready to hand which sustains
the moral values that favor limiting the population while
still safeguarding the environment. Namely, it is a matter
of respecting the future interests of people now unborn, but
only of future actual people. We recognize no present unactualized possibilities.

Thus we do what we can with our ultimate values, but we
have to deplore the irreparable lack of the empirical checkpoints that are the solace of the scientist. Loose ends are untidy at best, and disturbingly so when the ultimate good is
at stake.

7

Five Milestones
of Empiricism

In the past two centuries there have been five points where empiricism has taken a turn for the better. The first is the shift from ideas to words. The second is the shift of semantic focus from terms to sentences. The third is the shift of semantic focus from sentences to systems of sentences. The fourth is, in Morton White's phrase, methodological monism: abandonment of the analytic-synthetic dualism. The fifth is naturalism: abandonment of the goal of a first philosophy prior to natural science. I shall proceed to elaborate on each of the five.

The first was the shift of attention from ideas to words. This was the adoption of the policy, in epistemology, of talking about linguistic expressions where possible instead of ideas. This policy was of course pursued by the medieval nominalists, but I think of it as entering modern empiricism only in 1786, when the philologist John Horne Tooke wrote as follows: "The greatest part of Mr. Locke's essay, that is, all which relates to what he calls the abstraction, complexity, generalization, relation, etc., of ideas, does indeed merely concern language" (p. 32).

This essay is part of a paper that I presented under the title "The pragmatists' place in empiricism" at a symposium at the University of South Carolina in 1975. The paper will be published by the University of South Carolina Press in the symposium volume *Pragmatism, Its Sources and Prospects*.

British empiricism was dedicated to the proposition that
only sense makes sense. Ideas were acceptable only if based
on sense impressions. But Tooke appreciated that the *idea*
idea itself measures up poorly to empiricist standards.
Translated into Tooke's terms, then, the basic proposition of
British empiricism would seem to say that words make sense
only insofar as they are definable in sensory terms.

At this point, trouble arises over grammatical particles:
what of our prepositions, our conjunctions, our copula?
These are indispensable to coherent discourse, yet how are
they definable in sensory terms? John Horne Tooke adopted
a heroic line here, arguing that the particles were really
ordinary concrete terms in degenerate form. He advanced
ingenious etymologies: 'if' was 'give', 'but' was 'be out'.
However, this line was needless and hopeless. If we could
make concrete terms do all the work of the grammatical
particles, we could make them do so without awaiting justification from etymologists. But surely we cannot, and there
is no valid reason to want to; for there is another approach
to the problem of defining the grammatical particles in sensory terms. We have only to recognize that they are *syncategorematic*. They are definable not in isolation but in context.

This brings us to the second of the five turning points, the
shift from terms to sentences. The medievals had the notion
of syncategorematic words, but it was a contemporary of
John Horne Tooke who developed it into an explicit theory
of contextual definition; namely, Jeremy Bentham. He applied contextual definition not just to grammatical particles
and the like, but even to some genuine terms, categorematic
ones. If he found some term convenient but ontologically em-
barrassing, contextual definition enabled him in some cases
to continue to enjoy the services of the term while disclaim-
ing its denotation. He could declare the term syncategorematic, despite grammatical appearances, and then could
justify his continued use of it if he could show systematically
how to paraphrase as wholes all sentences in which he chose
to imbed it. Such was his theory of fictions:[1] what he called
paraphrasis, and what we now call contextual definition. The

1. See Ogden.

term, like the grammatical particles, is meaningful as a part of meaningful wholes. If every sentence in which we use a term can be paraphrased into a sentence that makes good sense, no more can be asked.

Comfort could be derived from Bentham's doctrine of paraphrasis by all who may have inherited Berkeley's and Hume's misgivings over abstract ideas. Reconsidered in the spirit of John Horne Tooke, these misgivings become misgivings over abstract terms; and then Bentham's approach offers hope of accommodating such terms, in some contexts anyway, without conceding an ontology of abstract objects. I am persuaded that one cannot thus make a clean sweep of all abstract objects without sacrificing much of science, including classical mathematics. But certainly one can pursue those nominalistic aims much further than could have been clearly conceived in the days before Bentham and Tooke.

Contextual definition precipitated a revolution in semantics: less sudden perhaps than the Copernican revolution in astronomy, but like it in being a shift of center. The primary vehicle of meaning is seen no longer as the word, but as the sentence. Terms, like grammatical particles, mean by contributing to the meaning of the sentences that contain them. The heliocentrism propounded by Copernicus was not obvious, and neither is this. It is not obvious because, for the most part, we understand sentences only by construction from understood words. This is necessarily so, since sentences are potentially infinite in variety. We learn some words in isolation, in effect as one-word sentences; we learn further words in context, by learning various short sentences that contain them; and we understand further sentences by construction from the words thus learned. If the language that we thus learn is afterward compiled, the manual will necessarily consist for the most part of a word-by-word dictionary, thus obscuring the fact that the meanings of words are abstractions from the truth conditions of sentences that contain them.

It was the recognition of this semantic primacy of sentences that gave us contextual definition, and vice versa. I attributed this to Bentham. Generations later we find Frege

celebrating the semantic primacy of sentences, and Russell
giving contextual definition its fullest exploitation in technical logic. But Bentham's contribution had not been lying
ineffective all that while. In the course of the nineteenth
century a practice emerged in the differential calculus of
using differential operators as simulated coefficients while
recognizing that the operators were really intelligible only
as fragments of larger terms. It was this usage, indeed,
rather than Bentham's writings, that directly inspired Russell's contextual definitions.[2]

In consequence of the shift of attention from term to sentence, epistemology came in the twentieth century to be a
critique not primarily of concepts but of truths and beliefs.
The verification theory of meaning, which dominated the
Vienna Circle, was concerned with the meaning and meaningfulness of sentences rather than of words. The English
philosophers of ordinary language have likewise directed
their analyses to sentences rather than to words, in keeping
with the example that was set by both the earlier and the
later work of their mentor Wittgenstein. Bentham's lesson
penetrated and permeated epistemology in the fullness of
time.

The next move, number three in my five, shifts the focus
from sentences to systems of sentences. We come to recognize that in a scientific theory even a whole sentence is ordinarily too short a text to serve as an independent vehicle of
empirical meaning. It will not have its separable bundle of
observable or testable consequences. A reasonably inclusive
body of scientific theory, taken as a whole, will indeed have
such consequences. The theory will imply a lot of observation conditionals, as I call them,[3] each of which says that if
certain observable conditions are met then a certain observable event will occur. But, as Duhem has emphasized,
these observation conditionals are implied only by the theory
as a whole. If any of them proves false, then the theory is
false, but on the face of it there is no saying which of the
component sentences of the theory to blame. The observation
conditionals cannot be distributed as consequences of the

2. See Whitehead and Russell, 2d ed., p. 24.
3. See Essay 2 above.

several sentences of the theory. A single sentence of the theory is apt not to imply any of the observation conditionals.

The scientist does indeed test a single sentence of his theory by observation conditionals, but only through having chosen to treat that sentence as vulnerable and the rest, for the time being, as firm. This is the situation when he is testing a new hypothesis with a view to adding it, if he may, to his growing system of beliefs.

When we look thus to a whole theory or system of sentences as the vehicle of empirical meaning, how inclusive should we take this system to be? Should it be the whole of science? or the whole of *a* science, a branch of science? This should be seen as a matter of degree, and of diminishing returns. All sciences interlock to some extent; they share a common logic and generally some common part of mathematics, even when nothing else. It is an uninteresting legalism, however, to think of our scientific system of the world as involved *en bloc* in every prediction. More modest chunks suffice, and so may be ascribed their independent empirical meaning, nearly enough, since some vagueness in meaning must be allowed for in any event.

It would also be wrong to suppose that *no* single sentence of a theory has its separable empirical meaning. Theoretical sentences grade off to observation sentences; observationality is a matter of degree, namely, the degree of spontaneous agreement that the sentence would command from present witnesses. And while it may be argued that even an observation sentence may be recanted in the light of the rest of one's theory, this is an extreme case and happily not characteristic. And in any event there will be single sentences at the other extreme—long theoretical ones—that surely have their separable empirical meaning, for we can make a conjunctive sentence of a whole theory.

Thus the holism that the third move brings should be seen only as a moderate or relative holism. What is important is that we cease to demand or expect of a scientific sentence that it have its own separable empirical meaning.

The fourth move, to methodological monism, follows closely on this holism. Holism blurs the supposed contrast between the synthetic sentence, with its empirical content, and the analytic sentence, with its null content. The organiz-

ing role that was supposedly the role of analytic sentences is
now seen as shared by sentences generally, and the empirical
content that was supposedly peculiar to synthetic sentences
is now seen as diffused through the system.

The fifth move, finally, brings naturalism: abandonment
of the goal of a first philosophy. It sees natural science as
an inquiry into reality, fallible and corrigible but not answerable to any supra-scientific tribunal, and not in need
of any justification beyond observation and the hypothetico-
deductive method. Naturalism has two sources, both negative. One of them is despair of being able to define theoretical
terms generally in terms of phenomena, even by contextual
definition. A holistic or system-centered attitude should suffice to induce this despair. The other negative source of
naturalism is unregenerate realism, the robust state of mind
of the natural scientist who has never felt any qualms beyond
the negotiable uncertainties internal to science. Naturalism
had a representative already in 1830 in the antimetaphy-
sician Auguste Comte, who declared that "positive philosophy" does not differ in method from the special sciences.

Naturalism does not repudiate epistemology, but assim-
ilates it to empirical psychology. Science itself tells us that
our information about the world is limited to irritations of
our surfaces, and then the epistemological question is in
turn a question within science: the question how we human
animals can have managed to arrive at science from such
limited information. Our scientific epistemologist pursues
this inquiry and comes out with an account that has a good
deal to do with the learning of language and with the neu-
rology of perception. He talks of how men posit bodies and
hypothetical particles, but he does not mean to suggest that
the things thus posited do not exist. Evolution and natural
selection will doubtless figure in this account, and he will
feel free to apply physics if he sees a way.

The naturalistic philosopher begins his reasoning within
the inherited world theory as a going concern. He tentatively
believes all of it, but believes also that some unidentified portions are wrong. He tries to improve, clarify, and understand the system from within. He is the busy sailor adrift on
Neurath's boat.

8

Russell's Ontological Development

The twentieth century began, as many of you know, in 1901. Russell was twenty-eight and had published three books: one on politics, one on mathematics, and one on philosophy. Late next summer the century will be two-thirds over. Russell's books have run to forty, and his philosophical influence, direct and indirect, over this long period has been unequaled.

Russell's name is inseparable from mathematical logic, which owes him much, and it was above all Russell who made that subject an inspiration to philosophers. The new logic played a part in the philosophical doctrines that Russell propounded during the second decade of this century—doctrines of unsensed sensa and perspectives, logical constructions and atomic facts. These doctrines affect our thinking today both directly and through supervening schools of thought. The impact of logical empiricism upon present-day philosophy is to an important degree Russell's impact at one remove, as the references in Carnap and elsewhere generously attest. Moreover, Wittgenstein's philosophy was an evolution from views that Russell and the young Wittgenstein had shared. The Oxford philosophy of ordinary language must admit, however bleakly, to a strong strain of Russell in its origins.

A symposium paper, reprinted from the *Journal of Philosophy* 63 (1966). A few lines have been dropped and others permuted because of coverage by Essay 7 above.

I think many of us were drawn to our profession by Russell's books. He wrote a spectrum of books for a graduated public, layman to specialist. We were beguiled by the wit and a sense of newfound clarity with respect to central traits of reality. We got memorable first lessons in relativity, elementary particles, infinite numbers, and the foundations of arithmetic. At the same time we were inducted into traditional philosophical problems such as that of the reality of matter and that of the reality of minds other than our own. For all this emergence of problems the overriding sense of newfound clarity was more than a match. In sophisticated retrospect we have had at points to reassess that clarity, but this was a sophistication that we acquired only after we were hooked.

Russell spoke not only to a broad public, but to a broad subject matter. The scatter of his first three books set a precedent to which his books of the next six decades conformed. Some treat of education, marriage, morals, and, as in the beginning, politics. I shall not venture to guess whether the world is better for having heeded Russell in these farther matters to the degree that it has, or whether it is better for not having heeded him more. Or both.

Instead I shall talk of Russell's ontological development. For I must narrow my scope somehow, and ontology has the virtue of being central and not unduly narrow. Moreover, Russell's ontology was conditioned conspicuously by both his theory of knowledge and his logic.

In *Principles of Mathematics*, 1903, Russell's ontology was unrestrained. Every word referred to something. If the word was a proper name, in Russell's somewhat deviant sense of that phrase, its object was a *thing*; otherwise a *concept*. He limited the term 'existence' to things, but reckoned things liberally, even including instants and points of empty space. And then, beyond existence, there were the rest of the entities: "numbers, the Homeric gods, relations, chimeras, and four-dimensional spaces" (p. 449). The word 'concept', which Russell applied to these nonexistents, connotes mereness; but let us not be put off. The point to notice, epithets aside, is that gods and chimeras are as real for Russell as numbers. Now this is an intolerably indiscriminate ontology.

Take impossible numbers: prime numbers divisible by 6. It must in some sense be false that there are such; and this must be false in some sense in which it is true that there are prime numbers. In this sense are there chimeras? Are chimeras then as firm as the good prime numbers and firmer than the primes divisible by 6?

Russell may have meant to admit certain chimeras (the possible ones) to the realm of being, and still exclude the primes divisible by 6 as impossibles. Or he may, like Meinong, have intended a place even for impossible objects. I do not see that in *Principles of Mathematics* Russell faced that question.

Russell's long article on Meinong came out in *Mind* in installments the following year. In it he criticized details of Meinong's system, but still protested none against the exuberance of Meinong's realm of being. In the same quarterly three issues later, however, a reformed Russell emerges: the Russell of "On Denoting" (1905), fed up with Meinong's impossible objects. The reform was no simple change of heart; it hinged on Russell's discovery of a means of dispensing with the unwelcome objects. The device was Russell's theory of singular descriptions, that paradigm, as Ramsey has said, of philosophical analysis. It involved defining a term not by presenting a direct equivalent of it, but by what Bentham called *paraphrasis:* by providing equivalents of all desired sentences containing the term.[1] In this way, reference to fictitious objects can be simulated in meaningful sentences without our being committed to the objects. Frege and Peano had allowed singular description the status of a primitive notation; only with Russell did it become an "incomplete symbol defined in use."

The new freedom that paraphrasis confers is our reward for recognizing that the unit of communication is the sentence and not the word. This point of semantical theory was long obscured by the undeniable primacy, in one respect, of words. Sentences being limitless in number and words limited, we necessarily understand most sentences by construction from antecedently familiar words. Actually there

1. See Essay 7 above.

is no conflict here. We can allow the sentences a monopoly
of full "meaning," in some sense, without denying that the
meaning must be worked out. Then we can say that knowing
words is knowing how to work out the meanings of sentences
containing them. Dictionary definitions of words are mere
clauses in a recursive definition of the meanings of sentences.

Russell's preoccupation with incomplete symbols began
with his theory of singular descriptions in 1905. But it continued and spread, notably to classes. For background on
classes we must slip back a few years. Classes were an evident source of discomfort to Russell when he was writing
Principles of Mathematics. There was, for one thing, his
epoch-making paradox. Burali-Forti had found a paradox
of classes as early as 1897, but it concerned infinite ordinal
numbers, and could be accommodated, one hoped, by some
local adjustment of theory. On the other hand, Russell's
simple paradox of the class of all classes not belonging to
themselves struck at the roots. It dates from 1901, when, as
Frege expressed it to Russell, arithmetic tottered.

Russell's accommodation of the paradoxes, his theory of
types, came only in 1908. In *Principles*, 1903, we find no
more than tentative gropings in that direction. But *Principles* evinces much discomfort over classes also apart from
the paradoxes. The further source of discomfort is the ancient problem of the one and the many. It seems strange now
that Russell saw a problem in the fact that a single class
might have many members, since he evidently saw no problem in the corresponding fact that a single attribute, or
what he then called a class-concept, might apply to many
things. What made the difference was that, in the bipartite
ontology of *Principles of Mathematics*, classes counted as
things rather than as concepts; classes existed. Russell observed against Peano that "we must not identify the class
with the class-concept," because of extensionality: classes
with the same members are the same (p. 68). Since the class
was not the class-concept, Russell took it not to be a concept
at all; hence it had to be a thing. But then, he felt, it ought
to be no more than the sum of the things in it; and here was
his problem of the one and the many.

We saw that in 1905 Russell freed himself of Meinong's

impossibles and the like by a doctrine of incomplete symbols. Classes were next. In his 1908 paper, "Mathematical Logic as Based on the Theory of Types," there emerges not only the theory of types but also a doctrine of incomplete symbols for explaining classes away. This latter doctrine is designed precisely to take care of the point Russell had made against Peano in connection with extensionality. Russell's contextual definition of class notation gave the benefit of classes, namely, extensionality, without assuming more than class-concepts after all.

Seeing Russell's perplexities over classes, we can understand his gratification at accommodating classes under a theory of incomplete symbols. But the paradoxes, which were the most significant of these perplexities, were not solved by his theory of incomplete symbols; they were solved, or parried, by his theory of types. One is therefore startled when Russell declares in "My Mental Development" that his expedient of incomplete symbols "made it possible to see, in a general way, how a solution of the contradictions might be possible."[2] If the paradoxes had invested only classes and not class-concepts, then Russell's elimination of classes would indeed have eliminated the paradoxes and there would have been no call for the theory of types. But the paradoxes apply likewise, as Russell knew, to class-concepts, or propositional functions. And thus it was that the theory of types, in this its first full version of 1908, was developed expressly and primarily for propositional functions and then transmitted to classes only through the contextual definitions.

The startling statement that I quoted can be accounted for. It is linked to the preference that Russell was evincing, by 1908, for the phrase 'propositional function' over 'class-concept'. Both phrases were current in *Principles of Mathematics;* mostly the phrase 'propositional function' was visibly meant to refer to notational forms, namely, open sentences, while concepts were emphatically not notational. But after laying waste Meinong's realm of being in 1905, Russell trusted concepts less and favored the more nominalistic tone of the phrase 'propositional function', which bore the double

2. Schilpp, *Philosophy of Bertrand Russell*, p. 14.

burden. If we try to be as casual about the difference between use and mention as Russell was fifty and sixty years ago, we can see how he might feel that, whereas a theory of types of real classes would be ontological, his theory of types of propositional functions had a notational cast. Insofar, his withdrawal of classes would be felt as part of his solution of the paradoxes. This feeling could linger to 1943, when he wrote "My Mental Development," even if its basis had lapsed.

We, careful about use and mention, can tell when Russell's so-called propositional functions must be taken as concepts, more specifically as attributes and relations, and when they may be taken as mere open sentences or predicates. It is when he quantifies over them that he reifies them, however unwittingly, as concepts. This is why no more can be claimed for his elimination of classes than I claimed for it above: a derivation of classes from attributes, or concepts, by a contextual definition framed to supply the missing extensionality. On later occasions Russell writes as if he thought that his 1908 theory, which reappeared in *Principia Mathematica,* disposed of classes in some more sweeping sense than reduction to attributes.

Just how much more sweeping a reduction he was prepared to claim may have varied over the years. Hahn and other readers have credited him with explaining classes away in favor of nothing more than a nominalistic world of particulars and notations. But Russell early and late has expressly doubted the dispensability of universals. Even if we were ingeniously to paraphrase all talk of qualities, for instance, into an idiom in which we talk rather of similarity to chosen particulars instancing those qualities, still, Russell more than once remarked, we should be left with one universal, the relation of similarity. Now here, in contrast to the class matter, I think Russell even concedes the Platonists too much; retention of the two-place predicate 'is similar to' is no evidence of assuming a corresponding abstract entity, the similarity relation, as long as that relation is not invoked as a value of a bound variable. A moral of all this is that inattention to referential semantics works two ways, obscuring some ontological assumptions and creating an illusion of others.

What I have ascribed to confusion can be ascribed to in-difference; for we are apt to take pains over a distinction only to the degree that we think it matters. Questions as to what there is were for Russell of two sorts: questions of existence in his restricted sense of the term, and residual questions of being—questions of what he came to call 'subsistence'. The questions as to what subsists evidently struck him as less substantial, more idly verbal perhaps, than questions as to what exists. This bias toward the existential would explain his indiscriminate bestowal of subsistence in *Principles of Mathematics*. True, he called a halt in 1905 with his theory of descriptions; but on that occasion he was provoked by the impossibility of Meinong's impossibles. And he had even put up with those for a time. Moreover, Russell continued to be very prodigal with subsistence even after propounding his theory of descriptions. We find him saying still in 1912 that "nearly all the words to be found in the dictionary stand for universals."[3]

I am suggesting that through his fourth decade Russell took a critical interest in existential questions but was relatively offhand about subsistential ones. This bias explains his glee over eliminating classes and his indifference over the status of the surviving propositional functions; for we saw that in *Principles* the classes occupied, however uneasily, the existential zone of being. To hold that classes, if there be any, must exist, while attributes at best subsist, does strike me as arbitrary; but such was Russell's attitude.

Russell's relative indifference to subsistence shows again in his treatment of meaning. Frege's three-way distinction between the expression, what it means, and what if anything it refers to, did not come naturally to Russell. In "On Denoting," 1905, he even argued against it. His argument is hard to follow; at points it seems to turn on a confusion of expressions with their meanings, and at points it seems to turn on a confusion of the expression with the mention of it, while elsewhere in the same pages Russell seems clear on both distinctions. The upshot is that "the relation of '*C*' to *C* remains wholly mysterious; and where are we to find the

3. *Problems of Philosophy*, p. 146.

denoting complex '*C*' which is supposed to denote *C?* . . . This
is an inextricable tangle, and seems to prove that the whole
distinction between meaning and denotation has been
wrongly conceived."

In other writings Russell commonly uses the word 'meaning' in the sense of 'reference'; thus " 'Napoleon' means a
certain individual" and " 'Man' means a whole class of such
particulars as have proper names."[4] What matters more
than terminology is that Russell seldom seems heedful,
under any head, of a subsistent entity such as *we* might call
the meaning, over and above the existent object of reference.
He tends, as in the 1905 paper "On Denoting," to blur that
entity with the expression itself. Such was his general tendency with subsistents.

For my own part, I am chary of the idea of meaning, and,
furthermore, I think Russell too prodigal with subsistent
entities. So it would be odd of me to criticize Russell for not
recognizing meanings as subsistent entities. However, the
outcome that wants criticizing is just that, for want of distinctions, Russell tended to blur meaninglessness with failure
of reference. This was why he could not banish the king of
France without first inventing the theory of descriptions. To
make sense is to have a meaning, and the meaning is the
reference; so 'the king of France' is meaningless and 'The
king of France is bald' is meaningful only by being short for
a sentence not containing 'the king of France'. Well, even if
the theory of descriptions was not needed in quite this way,
it brought major clarifications and we are thankful for it.

Russell's tendency to blur subsistent entities with expressions was noticed in his talk of propositional functions. It is
equally noticeable in what he says of propositions. In *Principles of Mathematics* he describes propositions as expressions, but then he speaks also of the unity of propositions
(p. 50), and of the possibility of infinite propositions (p.
145), in ways ill suited to such a version. In "Meinong's Theory," 1904, he speaks of propositions as judgments (p. 523).
There is similar oscillation in *Principia Mathematica*.

But by the time of "The Philosophy of Logical Atomism,"

4. *Analysis of Mind*, pp. 191, 194.

1918, the oscillation has changed direction. At one point in this essay we read, "a proposition is just a symbol" (p. 185) ; at a later point we read rather, "Obviously propositions are nothing . . . To suppose that in the actual world of nature there is a whole set of false propositions going about is to my mind monstrous" (p. 223). This repudiation is startling. We had come to expect a blur between expressions and subsistent entities, concepts; what we get instead of subsistence is nothingness. The fact is that Russell has stopped talking of subsistence. He stopped by 1914. What would once have counted as subsisting has been disposed of in any of three ways: identified with its expression, or repudiated utterly, or elevated to the estate of out-and-out existence. Qualities and relations come to enjoy this elevation; Russell speaks in "The Philosophy of Logical Atomism" of "those ultimate simples, out of which the world is built, . . . that . . . have a kind of reality not belonging to anything else. Simples . . . are of an infinite number of sorts. There are particulars and qualities and relations of various orders, a whole hierarchy" (p. 270).

Russell's abandonment of the term 'subsistence' was an improvement. It is a quibbling term; its function is to limit existence verbally to space-time and so divert attention from ontological commitments of other than spatio-temporal kind. Better to acknowledge all posits under an inclusive and familiar heading. Posits too dubious for such recognition will then be dropped, as were propositions in some sense.

As for propositions, in particular, we saw Russell in this essay taking them as expressions part of the time and part of the time simply repudiating them. Dropping then the ambiguous epithet, we might take this to be Russell's net thought: there are no nonlinguistic things that are somehow akin to sentences and asserted by them.

But this is not Russell's thought. In the same essay he insists that the world does contain nonlinguistic things that are akin to sentences and asserted by them; he merely does not call them propositions. He calls them facts. It turns out that the existence of nonlinguistic analogues of sentences offends Russell only where the sentences are false. His facts are what many of us would have been content to call true propositions. Russell himself called them that in 1904,[5] propositions then being judgments; and in the 1918 essay now under discussion he allows them full-fledged existence. "Facts belong to the objective world" (p. 183). True, he says a page earlier that "when I speak of a fact I do not mean a particular existing thing"; but he is here distinguishing between fact and thing only as between sorts of existents, paralleling the distinction between sentences and names. Facts you can assert and deny; things you can name (p. 270). Both exist; 'thing' has ceased to be coextensive with 'existent'.

Russell in this 1918 essay acknowledges Wittgenstein's influence. Russell's ontology of facts here is a reminder of Wittgenstein, but a regrettable one. Wittgenstein thought in his *Tractatus* days that true sentences mirrored nature, and this notion led him to posit things in nature for true sentences to mirror; namely, facts.

Not that Wittgenstein started Russell on facts. Russell was urging a correspondence between facts and propositions in 1912,[6] when he first knew Wittgenstein; and he equates facts with true judgments as early, we saw, as 1904. Russell had his own reason for wanting facts as entities, and Wittgenstein abetted him.

Russell was receptive to facts as entities because of his tendency to conflate meaning with reference. Sentences, being meaningful, had to stand to some sort of appropriate entities in something fairly like the relation of naming. Propositions in a nonsentential sense were unavailable, having been repudiated; so facts seemed all the more needed. They do not exactly serve as references of false sentences, but they help. For each true or false sentence there *is* a fact, which the sentence asserts or denies according as the sentence is true or false. This two-to-one variety of reference became for Russell even a central trait distinguishing sentences from names, and so facts from things.[7]

Russell continued to champion facts, right through his *In-*

5. "Meinong's theory," p. 523.
6. *Problems of Philosophy*, pp. 198ff.
7. "Philosophy of logical atomism," pp. 187, 270.

quiry into Meaning and Truth and into *Human Knowledge,* 1948. In *Human Knowledge* the term applies not only to what true statements assert, but to more: "Everything that there is in the world I call a 'fact' " (p. 143).

Russell's predilection for a fact ontology depended, I suggested, on confusion of meaning with reference. Otherwise I think Russell would have made short shrift of facts. He would have been put off by what strikes a reader of "The Philosophy of Logical Atomism": how the analysis of facts rests on analysis of language. Anyway Russell does not admit facts as fundamental; atomic facts are atomic as facts go, but they are compound objects.[8] The atoms of Russell's logical atomism are not atomic facts but sense data.

In *Problems of Philosophy,* 1912, Russell had viewed both sense data and external objects as irreducible existents. We are acquainted with sense data beyond peradventure, he held, whereas our belief in external objects is fallible; still, speaking fallibly, both are real. Our belief in external objects is rooted in instinct, but it is rational of us, he held, to accept such dictates of instinct in the absence of counter-evidence (p. 39). This cheerful resignation echoes Hume and harmonizes also with the current Oxford way of justifying scientific method: scientific method is part of what 'rational' means.

Two years later, in *Our Knowledge of the External World,* Russell was more sanguine. Here it was that sense data became logical atoms for the construction of the rest of the world. Already in *Problems* he had talked of private worlds of sense data and the public space of physics, and of their correlations. Now we find him using these correlations as a means of identifying external objects with classes of sense data. He identifies the external object with the class of all the views of it in private worlds, actual and ideal. In so doing he also pinpoints each of the private worlds as a point in public space.

It was a great idea. If executed with all conceivable success, it would afford translation of all discourse about the

8. "Philosophy of logical atomism," pp. 195f, 270; *Our Knowledge of the External World,* p. 54.

external world into terms of sense data, set theory, and logic. It would not settle induction, for we should still be in the position of predicting sense data from sense data. But it would settle the existence of external things. It would show that assumption superfluous, or prove it true; we could read the result either way.

It would neatly settle the ontology of the external world, by reducing it to that of the set theory of sense data. In *Our Knowledge of the External World,* moreover, Russell wrote as though he had eliminated classes, and not just reduced them to attributes (see pp. 224f); so he would have looked upon the project, if successful, as resting on an ontology of sense data alone (see p. 153). But by 1918 he thought better of this point, as witness the recognition of "qualities and relations . . . a whole hierarchy" lately quoted.

In *Our Knowledge of the External World* Russell expressed no confidence that the plan he sketched could be fully realized. In his sketch, as he remarked, he took other minds for granted; moreover, he broached none of the vast detail that would be needed for the further constructions, except for a few illustrative steps. But the illustrations gave a vivid sense that the concepts of *Principia Mathematica* could be helpful here and the many ingenious turns and strategies of construction that went into *Principia* could be imitated to advantage. A strategy much in evidence is definition by abstraction—what Whitehead came to call *extensive abstraction,* and Carnap *quasi-analysis.*

It was left to Carnap, in 1928, to be inspired to press the plan. Russell's intervening works, "The Philosophy of Logical Atomism," *Analysis of Matter,* and *Analysis of Mind* might in view of their titles have been expected to further it, but they did not. The dazzling sequel to *Our Knowledge of the External World* was rather Carnap's *Der logische Aufbau der Welt.* Carnap achieved remarkable feats of construction, starting with sense data and building explicitly, with full *Principia* techniques and *Principia* ingenuity, toward the external world. One must in the end despair of the full definitional reduction dreamed of in recent paragraphs, and it is one of the merits of the *Aufbau* that we can see from it where the obstacles lie. The worst obstacle seems to be that the assigning of sense qualities to public place-times has to be kept open to revision in the light of later experience, and so cannot be reduced to definition. The empiricist's regard for experience thus impedes the very program of reducing the world to experience.[9]

Russell meanwhile was warping his logical atomism over from its frankly phenomenalistic form to what, influenced by Perry and Holt, he called "neutral monism."[10] Neutrality here has a bias, as it often has in politics; Russell's neutral particulars are on the side of sense data. Still, a drift has begun, and it continues. It does not reach the physicalistic pole, even in *Human Knowledge;* but there is an increasing naturalism, an increasing readiness to see philosophy as natural science trained upon itself and permitted free use of scientific findings. Russell had stated the basis for such an attitude already in 1914: "There is not any superfine brand of knowledge, obtainable by the philosopher, which can give us a standpoint from which to criticize the whole of the knowledge of daily life. The most that can be done is to examine and purify our common knowledge by an internal scrutiny, assuming the canons by which it has been obtained."[11]

9. This ironic way of putting the matter is due to Burton Dreben.
10. Cf. *Analysis of Mind*, p. 25; *Analysis of Matter*, ch. 37.
11. *Our Knowledge of the External World*, p. 71.

On Austin's Method

Once there were but a handful of therapeutic positivists and a multitude of chronic metaphysicians. Now there are therapists in every college. The epidemic has been stemmed and the therapy is routine. How are the veteran therapists hereafter to occupy their minds? One way is by directing their efforts against a continuing but less virulent form of the infection, namely, against philosophical perplexity in the lay mind. Ryle in his *Dilemmas* had a successful go at this. Another way is by continuing the kind of language study that went into the therapy, but continuing it now as a line of pure research. Characteristic writings of Austin's seem to fit in here.

Austin's technique, as Urmson has described it in this symposium, is a mode of introspective inquiry into semantics, conducted by native speakers in groups. It is an inquiry that is continuous with portions of linguistics, and probably capable both of benefiting from professional work in that field and of supplementing it. Despite its philosophical antecedents, it is an inquiry whose affinities in linguistics are not in theoretical linguistics; they are in lexicography. It is an inquiry into subtle differences in the semantics, or circumstances of use, of selected English phrases.

Semantic theory is plagued by the lack of an acceptable

A résumé of this symposium paper appeared in the *Journal of Philosophy* 62 (1965), and the whole in K. T. Fann, ed., *Symposium on J. L. Austin* (London: Routledge, 1969).

general definition of meaning. A definition of meaning simply as circumstances of use is inadequate because of vagueness as to how much may relevantly be included under 'circumstances'. However, that general problem of demarcating the circumstances is a problem that plagues semantic theory and not lexicographic practice, or, in particular, Austin's kind of inquiry. As long as one limits oneself to volunteering specific circumstances of use of expressions, the problem of meaning does not arise. There is a certain immunity in the concrete case.

The nature of this immunity may be clarified by an analogy from proof theory. Consider the notion of a mechanical method. In order to prove or even clearly state Gödel's theorem of the incompletability of number theory, or Church's theorem of the undecidability of quantification theory, we have to define the notion of a mechanical method; and recursiveness was the answer. But in showing the decidability of a theory we need no definition of mechanical method; we just present a method which everyone would call mechanical. Similarly Austin was able to present specific circumstances of use without broaching the problem of meaning.

For that matter, the same can be said of what Carnap calls explication—the sort of conceptual reduction that figures prominently in the philosophy of mathematics and elsewhere. Each explication stands on its own merits, without broaching the general problem of synonymy or meaning. But I digress.

Austin's manner of semantic inquiry contrasts with main trends in linguistics in being avowedly introspective. Any linguist certainly introspects his language much of the time, but Austin was unusual in adhering to introspective data exclusively. Such data are said to be untrustworthy because of their subjectivity, but, as Urmson explained, Austin had an ingenious remedy for that: he gained objectivity by group introspection.

This remedy is an instance of a perhaps more widely useful strategy. In its general form the strategy consists in exploiting the subjective and then objectifying it afterward by a social summation over individual subjects. The strategy

has uses also apart from the introspective situation. Thus
suppose some exotic field linguist from overseas were here
testing us to see what things we apply various terms to. He
would find, by induction from sample tests, that each of us
will apply the term 'pup' on sight to just the things to which
each of us will apply 'young dog'. In this way he will discover that our terms 'pup' and 'young dog' are coextensive.
But he could not, by that method, equate 'bachelor' with 'unmarried man'; for no two of us will even apply 'bachelor'
on sight to all and only the same persons, let alone 'unmarried man', given our differences in acquaintance and information. However, our visiting linguist can still equate
'bachelor' with 'unmarried man' after all if he resorts to
the strategy of first studying each subject in isolation and
only afterward objectifying by a social summation. He will
find that each of us will apply 'bachelor' just when *he* will
apply 'unmarried man'.

Let me broach next the utterly boring question, as Urmson
called it, of how to classify Austin's introspective semantics.
Is it to be called philosophy? To call it that does not, from
Austin's point of view as described by Urmson, say much
about it; philosophy is "a heterogeneous set of enquiries." I
applaud this casual attitude toward the demarcation of disciplines. Names of disciplines should be seen only as technical aids in the organization of curricula and libraries; a
scholar is better known by the individuality of his problems
than by the name of his discipline. If deans and librarians
class some of his problems as philosophical, that is no reason
for him to be concerned with other problems that they class
as philosophical: his further concerns might just as well be
problems that are classed as linguistic or mathematical. For
that matter, naming disciplines even fosters philosophical
error. To take the most glaring case, why do people insist on
viewing all parts of physics, however theoretical, as in some
degree empirical, and all parts of mathematics, however
practical, as purely formal? No such contrast would emerge
sentence by sentence, or problem by problem, without reference to the nominal demarcation of disciplines. But again I
digress.

Does calling Austin's distinctive activity philosophical say

anything about it? The one salient trait of philosophical in-
quiries, according to Austin as represented by Urmson, is
that for want of standard methods they have not yet hived
off under some special name. This criterion is not helpful.
The want of standard methods in Austin's work is surely not
so dire as to prevent its hiving off under the special name
of linguistics.

Actually Austin's work has a genuine tie to philosophy,
in a more substantial sense than just what hasn't hived off.
It cames in his choice of idioms for analysis. He was no
Baconian inductivist, amassing random samples of the world
or of the dictionary and scanning them with untendentious
eye for unpreconceived uniformities. The *arrière pensée* of
How to Do Things with Words emerges toward the end of
that book: it is "an inclination to play Old Harry with . . .
(1) the true/false fetish, (2) the value/fact fetish" (p. 150).

That book would have been different, in respect of one of
its avowed motives at any rate, if Austin had appreciated
Tarski's work on truth. Ironically, I think it was overattention to a demarcation of disciplines that deprived him of
Tarski's insights. It was overattention to the demarcation
of the study of English usage. But this in turn was due, I
think, to a basic impatience with philosophical perplexity.

There are two ways of rising to problems. Thus take the
perturbations of Mercury. I suppose that before Einstein
some astronomers pondered these with an eager curiosity,
hoping that they might be a key to important traits of nature
hitherto undetected, while other astronomers saw in them
a vexatious anomaly and longed to see how to explain them
away in terms of instrumental error. Attitudes toward philosophical problems vary similarly, and Austin's was of the
negative kind. Hence his tendency to limit a philosophical
venture to the study of word usage; for language criticism
was the method of therapeutic positivism, the method of the
Ueberwindung der Metaphysik.

What counts as true even for Tarski's theory of truth is
language, granted. But the value of Tarski's theory stands
forth only if at the second level, talking *of* truth, we look
beyond language to logic.

In his scintillating essay "Truth," Austin himself went

part way down Tarski's path. In a footnote he even cited Tarski's paradigm, " 'It is raining' is true if and only if it is raining," and commented: "So far so good." Then he looked into usage to add to the story. Tarski, in contrast, concentrated on the mathematical significance of his paradigm. For all its surface triviality, the paradigm is quickly shown to have extraordinary powers. For one thing, it suffices, of itself, to determine truth uniquely. If there are two truth predicates 'True$_1$' and 'True$_2$', both fulfilling the paradigm, then the two are coextensive. More remarkable still, as Tarski showed, not even one truth predicate can quite fulfill the paradigm, on pain of contradiction. Yet, as he went on to show in the more laborious stretches of his "Wahrheitsbegriff," a predicate fulfilling the paradigm can after all be constructed suitable to any preassigned language that is fixed in vocabulary and formal in its logical structure, provided that we bring to the construction certain set-theoretic aids from beyond the bounds of the preassigned language itself. A conclusion that follows from all this is the openness of set theory: for each consistent set theory there is a stronger. This follows also from Gödel's work; and Tarski's work strikingly illuminates Gödel's.

The problem of the perturbations of Mercury turned out to be one of the keys to the relativity of space and time, and the problem of truth turned out to be one of the keys to the relativity of set theories.

I quoted Austin as saying that *How to Do Things with Words* was prompted in part by an animus against the true/false fetish. Yet the relevance of the book to the fetish is not clear, if we think of truth in terms of Tarski's paradigm. The paradigm works for evaluations, after all, as Smart has noticed (1965), as well as for statements of fact. And it works equally for performatives. 'Slander is evil' is true if and only if slander is evil, and 'I bid you good morning' is true of us on a given occasion if and only if, on that occasion, I bid you good morning. A performative is a notable sort of utterance, I grant; it makes itself true; but then it is true. There are good reasons for contrasting and comparing performatives and statements of fact, but an animus against the true/false fetish is not one of them.

Developments in *How to Do Things with Words* that were
prompted directly or indirectly by Austin's animus against
the true/false fetish are best understood rather as explora-
tions of the gulf between sentence and statement. His work
on this will doubtless be continued by others. As for "the
value/fact fetish," his work seems rather to depict the inter-
twining of value and fact than to discredit the distinction—
though someone may discredit it. Anyway his inclination to
play Old Harry with those two fetishes has issued in percep-
tive work that should be relevant to the philosophy of law
and other domains.

Historians of science tell us that science forges ahead not
by an indiscriminate Baconian inductivism but by pursuing
preconceptions, even mistaken ones. I see in Austin's work
this kind of progress.

10

Smart's Philosophy and Scientific Realism

The Oxford-style philosopher, so influential nowadays, turns his good ear to the dictates of unspoiled common sense and his other to science. Historians of science itself, not to be outdone, take to belittling the force of evidence and saying how fashion spins the plot. Even leading quantum physicists have been known to impute reality primarily to ordinary things, their experimental equipment, as against the diminutive objects of their theory.

In refreshing contrast, South Australia's professor of philosophy J. J. C. Smart propounds in *Philosophy and Scientific Realism* "an unashamedly realistic view of the fundamental particles of physics . . . Indeed," he pursues, "I would wish to go further than merely to defend the physicist's picture of the world as an ontologically respectable one. I would wish to urge that the physicist's language gives us a *truer* picture of the world than does the language of ordinary common sense" (pp. 18, 47). With science dominating our lives and progressing ever faster on ever more frontiers, it is strange that such a view needs urging. Strange but true.

In fact, Smart declares not just for science but for physics. There have been materialists who held that living things,

Reprinted with permission from *The New York Review of Books*, July 9, 1964. Copyright © 1964 Nyrev, Inc.

though material, were subject to biological and psychological laws that were irreducible in principle to laws of physics. Such was the materialism of emergence. Smart's materialism is more robust.

Seeing how right-minded the book is, how congenial to one's own way of thinking, one expects its value to lie rather in persuading others than in instructing oneself. But on this score there are pleasant surprises. One of them comes on the heels of Smart's denial of emergence in biology and psychology. "Not only do I deny the existence of emergent laws and properties," he writes (p. 52), "but I even deny that in biology and psychology there are laws in the strict sense at all." The propositions of biology and psychology are local generalizations about some terrestrial growths of our acquaintance. In principle they are on a par with natural history and geography, or with consumers' reports. This is true, he urges, even of propositions about cell division. If they "are made universal in scope, then such laws are very likely not universally true. If they are not falsified by some queer species or phenomenon on earth they are very likely falsified elsewhere in the universe. The laws of physics, by contrast, seem to be truly universal" (pp. 54f).

Biology runs deeper, he grants, than cell division. There are the chromosome, the virus, the gene, nucleic acid, and the genetic code. Propositions on these matters are presumably broader in scope, admittedly more theoretical, and potentially more explanatory than other propositions in biology. Just so; and they are more nearly physico-chemical.

Physics investigates the essential nature of the world, and biology describes a local bump. Psychology, human psychology, describes a bump on the bump. Remarkable it is, and a matter of philosophical bemusement down the ages, that some parochial sensory responses and thought processes up in that bump of a bump should be equal to the physicist's business of encompassing the essential nature of the world. It takes an ingenious bit of triangulating from way off center.

This reflection goes well with a point that Smart makes about color. Color dominates our sensory experience; things that contrast in color are emphatically in contrast. Yet, and

here is Smart's point, color differences seldom bear interestingly upon physical laws. The reason is that a mixed
color can look to us like a pure one, and yet its looking like
that pure one hinges on special mechanisms in us which
could be otherwise and perhaps are otherwise in other creatures. "Extraterrestrial beings could be expected to have a
similar concept of length or electric charge to ours, but we
would not expect their colour concepts, supposing they had
any, to correspond to ours in any simple manner . . . To see
the world *sub specie aeternitatis* . . . we must eschew the concepts of colour and other secondary qualities" (p. 84).

It is along this line that Smart makes sense of the traditional philosophical distinction between primary and secondary qualities, and simultaneously accounts for its importance. The primary qualities—length, shape, weight,
hardness, and the like—are the ones that enter most simply
into physical laws.

Largely the book is given over to standard topics of controversy: physicalism versus phenomenalism, the mind-
body problem, man the machine, freedom and responsibility,
the reality of the future. I have hinted how the first one
comes out: physicalism wins. For arguments the reader is
referred to the book, and Godspeed. In each of these further
confrontations likewise, as the reader will have begun to
guess, right wins out: the body, the machine, responsibility,
the future.

In the mind-body affair it is restful to see mental states
identified unapologetically with bodily ones, and no semantic
hedging. There are answers, simply, to stock objections.

On man as machine, latter-day antimechanists have invoked Gödel's theorem, which says that no formal proof
procedure can encompass number theory. Smart, defending a
mechanistic view, takes issue with this rather wistful application of Gödel's great theorem. Where man rises above
the limitations of formal proof procedure, Smart suggests,
is in the informal and largely inconclusive maneuvers of scientific method; and a computing machine could in principle
be programmed to do the same.

Smart agrees with Hobbes that freedom and determinism are not antithetical; determined acts count as free when
mediated through the agent in certain ways. The division of

acts into some for which a man is regarded as responsible, and others for which he is not, is part of the social apparatus of reward and punishment: responsibility is allocated where rewards and punishments have tended to work as incentives and deterrents.

Such, in important part, is the use of "he could." There is also another use, as Smart observes: one which is on a par with "it could," as in "it could have broken." He links this use to incompleteness of information regarding the causal circumstances. I applaud this as a general attitude toward the modalities of possibility and necessity; they turn upon our own abstraction from particulars, for instance through our ignorance of them, rather than upon the nature of the world.

There is a conception, which Smart scouts, of the present moment as advancing through time at an inexorable pace of sixty seconds per minute. There is a notion also that sentences about the future are as yet neither true nor false, and that otherwise fatalism would reign and striving would be useless. These confusions are popular and in part Aristolelian. In the writings of Donald Williams (pp. 262–307) and others they have been set to rights with all clarity. Still, Smart adds distinctive touches in setting them to rights again. There incidentally emerges in the course of this exposition an arresting contrast between probability and truth. "Probable," he brings out, is an *indicator* word like 'I,' 'you,' 'now,' 'then,' 'here,' 'there': a word whose reference depends on the occasion of its use. For a statement of specific fact is true once and for all, if at all, whether we know it or not, but even so it may be more or less probable from occasion to occasion. The modality of probability ends up thus in a limbo of subjectivity, where the modalities of possibility and necessity just preceded it.

The book is couched in words unminced though uncontentious. A tendency to mince, in such right-minded writings, may be due in part to writers' awareness that people think these ideas are morally pernicious. But Smart handles this moral dilemma rather by taking it by the horns, in five final pages on materialism and values. I am happy to report that the materialist gains his moral victory hands down.

11

Goodman's Ways of Worldmaking

Ways of Worldmaking is a congeries. Not indeed an incongruous congeries, as of congers and costermongers, but withal a congeries to conjure with. For all its slenderness it offers us a philosophy of style, a philosophy of quotation, a philosophy of art, a philosophy of optical illusion, and a philosophy of nature. It is this last that packages the lot and gives it a name. The looseness of the package is in keeping with the philosophy that assembles it; for the doctrine is that there are many worlds, none all-embracing.

There is currently a Leibniz revival that has philosophers luxuriating in a continuum of possible worlds. One sterling virtue of Nelson Goodman's philosophy is that it is no part of that. Goodman means all his worlds to be actual. Proceeding then to try to penetrate what one hopes is a figure of speech, one finds that where the purported multiplicity really lies is not so much in worlds as in versions: world versions. I cannot quite say versions of the world, for Goodman holds that there is no one world for them to be versions of. He would sooner settle for the versions and let the world or worlds go by.

His doctrine rests partly on an appreciation of the creative component in natural science. Even the most rudimen-

---

Reprinted with permission from *The New York Review of Books*, November 23, 1978. Copyright © 1978 Nyrev, Inc.

tary of scientific laws is a generalization beyond the instances observed. There are divergent ways of generalizing from the same observations; some ways relatively simple, others arbitrarily gerrymandered.

We settle tentatively on the simplest one, but we may be forced off it by later observations. Even in observation itself there is a creative component: we overlook features irrelevant to our concerns, we perceive broad forms and gloss over discontinuities, we round out and round off. And at the other extreme, in the high flights of theoretical physics, man's creativity is overwhelming. Physical theory is indeed uncannily successful in the corroborations that it predicts and in the power over nature that it confers, but even so it is ninety-nine parts conceptualization to one part observation. May there not be some radically alternative conceptual structure, undreamt of, that would fit all the past observations and all the predicted ones equally well, and yet be untranslatable into our scheme? Our own physical theory and that one would be two world versions, equally sound. Two versions of *the* world? But what world is that? To describe it we must retreat into one or the other version; they share no neutral description. Recognize the two versions, Goodman says, and leave it at that.

This much will already estrange many of Goodman's readers. Not me. But then he presses on where I falter. Another world version that he treats with respect is the commonsense one which depicts a world not of atoms and electrons and nuclear particles but of sticks, stones, people, and other coarse objects. He sees further world versions, more fragmentary, in the styles of various painters. Thus he contrasts the world of Rembrandt with the world of Rouault and the world of Picasso. Shunning even the restraints of representational art, he forges on to abstract painting and to music: here again are world versions in their lesser ways. How, when they depict nothing? Well, they refer in another way: they stand as *samples* of interesting strains or qualities. There is a significant continuity, Goodman argues, between exemplification and depiction as well as between depiction and description.

One feels that this sequence of worlds or versions founders

in absurdity. I take Goodman's defense of it to be that there
is no reasonable intermediate point at which to end it. I
would end it after the first step: physical theory. I grant the
possibility of alternative physical theories, insusceptible to
adjudication; but I see the rest of his sequence of worlds or
world versions only as a rather tenuous metaphor.

Why, Goodman asks, this special deference to physical
theory? This is a good question, and part of its merit is that
it admits of a good answer. The answer is not that everything worth saying can be translated into the technical vocabulary of physics; not even that all good science can be
translated into that vocabulary. The answer is rather this:
nothing happens in the world, not the flutter of an eyelid,
not the flicker of a thought, without some redistribution of
microphysical states. It is usually hopeless and pointless to
determine just what microphysical states lapsed and what
ones supervened in the event, but some reshuffling at that
level there had to be; physics can settle for no less. If the
physicist suspected there was any event that did not consist
in a redistribution of the elementary states allowed for by
his physical theory, he would seek a way of supplementing
his theory. Full coverage in this sense is the very business
of physics, and only of physics.

Anyone who will say, "Physics is all very well in its place"
—and who will not?—is then already committed to a physicalism of at least the nonreductive, nontranslational sort
stated above. Hence my special deference to physical theory
as a world version, and to the physical world as the world.

Component essays in Goodman's congeries are rewarding
quite apart from the polycosmic motif that strings them together. There is a bright one on samples, which dramatizes
in deft parables the relation of sample to purpose. A swatch
represents its bolt in point of texture, pattern, and color,
but, unlike a sample cupcake, it deviates in size and shape.
But a swatch can also be used to exemplify swatches; and
then, he observes, its size and shape count for much and its
particular texture, pattern, and color for little.

The chapter on quotation explores the possibility of analogues of quotation, direct and indirect, in painting and
music. Goodman finds that depictions of picture frames will

not quite do as analogues of quotations marks, and that indirect quotation has better affinities in painting than direct.
Both sorts of quotation come off badly in music. The reasons
he gives for these similarities and contrasts afford some
worthwhile semantical insights.

The chapter on perception begins with the familiar illusion induced by closely paired flashes, which the eye per-
ceives as a single moving light. Remarkable variations of
this phenomenon are then reported, stemming from experiments by Paul Kolers. Illusions can be created of elaborate
permutations of position along quite unexpected lines, ac-
companied by changes of shape. Analogous affects are not
obtainable in the case of changes of color, and Goodman
offers an ingenious and convincing reason why they should
not be.

In his chapter on art he dismisses the traditional problem
of defining a work of art. He shows that the notion is hopelessly entangled with the fancied distinction in metaphysics
between internal and external relations, between intrinsic
and extrinsic, between essence and accident, which he laud-
ably rejects. He finds more significance in describing the
circumstances in which a thing functions as art; and it is as
a means to this venture that his discussion of swatches and
other samples fits in.

There are engaging passages. The scientist

seeks systems, simplicity, scope; and when satisfied on these scores
he tailors the truth to fit . . . He as much decrees as discovers the
laws he sets forth, as much designs as discerns the patterns he
delineates.

. . . we must distinguish falsehood and fiction from truth and
fact; but we cannot, I am sure, do it on the ground that fiction is
fabricated and fact found.

. . . the philosopher like the philanderer is always finding himself stuck with none or too many.

How can anyone this sensitive to words have coined
'acquacentric'? Why the Italian, or indeed anything to do
with Latin, when he could have played 'hydrocentric'
straight?

12

On the Individuation of Attributes

For a while I propose to treat tolerantly of attributes, or properties. Usually I have taken a harsher line. Classes, down the years, I have grudgingly admitted; attributes not. I have felt that if I must come to terms with Platonism, the least I can do is keep it extensional. For this brief space, however, it will be convenient to keep the question of the existence of attributes in abeyance, or even to talk as if they existed.

Attributes are classes with a difference. That is, corresponding to one and the same class there may be several *different* attributes. The point is that no two classes have exactly the same members, but two different attributes may be attributes of exactly the same things. Classes are identical when their members are identical; such is the principle of individuation of classes. On the other hand, attributes, I have often complained, have no clear principle of individuation.

Faulty individuation has nothing to do with vagueness of boundaries. We are accustomed to tolerating vagueness of boundaries. We have little choice in the matter. The boundaries of a desk are vague when we get down to the fine structure, because the clustering of the molecules grades off; the

Reprinted from A. R. Anderson, R. B. Marcus, and R. M. Martin, eds., *The Logical Enterprise: Essays for Frederick B. Fitch* (New Haven: Yale University Press, 1975).

allegiance of any particular peripheral molecule is indeterminate, as between the desk and the atmosphere. However, this vagueness of boundaries detracts none from the sharpness of our *individuation* of desks and other physical objects. What the vagueness of boundaries amounts to is this: there are many almost identical physical objects, almost coextensive with one another, and differing only in the inclusion or exclusion of various peripheral molecules. Any one of these almost coextensive objects could serve as the desk, and no one the wiser; such is the vagueness of the desk. Nevertheless they *all* have their impeccable principle of individuation; physical objects are identical if and only if coextensive. Where coextensiveness is not quite fully *verifiable,* neither is identity, but the identity is still well *defined,* though the desk is not. Specification is one thing, individuation another. Physical objects are well individuated, whatever else they are not. We know what it takes to distinguish them, even where we cannot detect it.

It then follows that the classes of physical objects are well individuated too, since their identity consists simply in the identity of the members. But what, on the other hand, is the principle of individuation of attributes? Thus grant me that any creature with a heart has kidneys and vice versa. The class of hearted creatures and the class of kidneyed creatures are identical. Still, we are not prepared to identify the attribute of heartedness with that of kidneyedness. Coextensiveness of attributes is not enough. What more, then, is wanted?

I forget who it was—let me call him Zedsky—that offered an interestingly exasperating answer to this question. The necessary and sufficient condition for identity of attributes is quite as clear, he contended, as the notions of class and member—notions with which I evidently have no quarrel. For we have only to look to Russell's general definition of identity, which explains identity for attributes and anything else. In general, objects x and y are identical if and only if they are members of just the same classes. So attributes, in particular, are identical if and only if they are members of exactly the same classes of attributes. This of course is an exasperating defense; but it is interesting to consider why.

We might object to Zedsky's answer in the following way. He says that attributes are identical when the classes that they belong to are identical. But when are such classes identical? They are classes of attributes. They are identical when their members are identical; that was the principle of individuation of classes. It was a good principle of individuation of classes of physical objects, since we had a good prior standard of identity of physical objects. But it is useless for classes of attributes; we cannot appeal to identity of the members, failing a prior standard of individuation of attributes, these being the members. Zedsky is evidently caught in a circle, individuating attributes in terms of identity of classes whose individuation depends on that of attributes.

Zedsky might answer in turn by protesting that the Russellian definition which he is applying to attributes does not really mention identity of classes. When expressed in words it seems to do so: attributes are identical when the classes that they belong to are identical. But it is simpler in symbols, and says nothing of identity of classes. What is required in order that attributes A and B be identical is simply that (z) $(A \in z .\equiv. B \in z)$. This formula contains only the single variable 'z' for classes of attributes, and no mention of identity.

What this shows is that we must look a little deeper. The real reason why the formula does not clarify the individuation of attributes is not that it mentions identity of classes of attributes, but that it mentions classes of attributes at all. We have an acceptable notion of class, or physical object, or attribute, or any other sort of object, only insofar as we have an acceptable principle of individuation for that sort of object. There is no entity without identity. But the individuation of classes of attributes depends, we saw, on the individuation of attributes. This, then, is why we are not satisfied with an account of the individuation of attributes which, like Zedsky's, depends on the notion of classes of attributes at all.

These thoughts on attributes remind us that classes themselves are satisfactorily individuated only in a relative sense. They are as satisfactorily individuated as their members.

Classes of physical objects are well individuated; so also, therefore, are classes of classes of physical objects; and so on up. Classes of attributes, on the other hand, are as badly off as attributes. The notion of a class of things makes no better sense than the notion of those things.

We may do well, with this relativism in mind, to cast an eye on the credentials of set theory. It turns out that the usual systems of set theory still stand up to the demands of individuation very well, if we assume that the ground elements or individuals of the system are physical objects or other well-individuated things rather than ill-individuated things such as attributes. For, we saw how classes of well-individuated things are well individuated; therefore so are classes of such classes; and so on up.

This takes care of the usual systems of set theory, which exclude *ungrounded* classes. A class is ungrounded if it has some member which has some member which . . . and so on downward *ad infinitum*, never reaching bottom. The system of my "New Foundations"[1] does have ungrounded classes, and so does the system of my *Mathematical Logic;* and it could be argued that for such classes there is no satisfactory individuation. They are identical if their members are identical, and these are identical if *their* members are identical, and there is no stopping. This, then, is a point in favor of the systems that bar ungrounded classes.

Our reflections on individuation have brought out a curious comparison of three grades of stringency. We can never quite specify the desk, from among various nearly coincident physical objects, because of vagueness at the edges. Yet its individuation, we saw, was quite in order. And we saw further that though with Zedsky we can define identity for attributes by applying Russell's general definition, still the individuation of attributes is not in order. These examples suggest that specification makes the most stringent demands, individuation is less stringent, and mere definition of identity is less stringent still.

I think I have adequately explained why Zedsky's account of the identity of attributes does not solve the problem of

---

1. Reprinted in *From a Logical Point of View*, pp. 80–101.

their individuation. But it may be worthwhile still, for the sake of a shift of perspective, to answer Zedsky again along a somewhat different line. For this we must consider sentences. How do we ever actually specify any particular attribute *or* any particular class? Or, for that matter, any particular proposition? Ordinarily, basically, we do so by citing an appropriate sentence. For specifying an attribute or a class it will be an open sentence, like '*x* has a heart,' giving the attribute of heartedness and the class of the hearted. For specifying a proposition it will be a closed sentence. Attributes, classes, and propositions are what we may call, in a word, *epiphrastic*. I am not saying that these entities are somehow ontologically dependent on sentences, or even that sentences can be formulated to fit all attributes or classes or propositions. I am saying how one ordinarily proceeds when one does succeed, if at all, in specifying any one attribute or class or proposition.

This being the case, the question of individuation of attributes becomes in practice a question of how to tell whether two open sentences express the same attribute. How should the two sentences be related? We may object to Zedsky that while his citation of Russell defines identity of attributes, it does not say how two sentences should be related in order to express an identical attribute. However, this objection needs tightening; he can rise to the new demand. By an easy adaptation of Russell's definition he can tell us how two sentences should be related. Thus let us represent the two sentences as '*Fx*' and '*Gx*', open sentences as they are. For '*Fx*' and '*Gx*' to express the same attribute, then, Zedsky can tell us, all that is required is that the attribute of being an *x* such that *Fx*, and the attribute of being an *x* such that *Gx*, belong to the same classes of attributes. In this rejoinder, Zedsky would simply be repeating the frustrating old Russell definition, but stretching it so as to squeeze the sentences '*Fx*' and '*Gx*' in, and thus meet our demand for a relation between sentences. Sentences '*Fx*' and '*Gx*' express the same attribute, so Zedsky would be telling us, just in case those sentences are so related that $(z) (x[Fx] \epsilon z .\equiv. x[Gx] \epsilon z)$.

What can we say to this? We have a pat answer, which we can carry over from the earlier argument. This is unsatisfactory in individuating attributes because, again, it assumes prior intelligibility of the notion of a class z of attributes. Indeed this is doubly unsatisfactory, for it assumes the notion of attribute also in the abstraction notation 'x[ ]', 'the attribute of being an x such that'.

So we now see that when we ask for a relation of sentences that will individuate attributes, we must require that the relation be expressed without mention of attributes. The notion of attribute is intelligible only insofar as we already know its principle of individuation.

Observe, in contrast, how well the corresponding requirement is met in the individuation of classes. I began by saying that classes are identical when their members are identical; but what we now want is a satisfactory formulation of a relation between two open sentences 'Fx' and 'Gx' which holds if and only if 'Fx' and 'Gx' determine the same class. The desired formulation is of course immediate: it is simply '$(x)(Fx \equiv Gx)$'. It does not talk of classes; it does not use class abstraction or epsilon, and it does not presuppose classes as values of variables. It is as pure as the driven snow. Classes, whatever their foibles, are the very model of individuation on this approach.

Can we do anything similar for attributes? Some say we can. Open sentences 'Fx' and 'Gx' express the same attribute, they say, if and only if they entail each other; if and only if the biconditional formed from them is analytic. Or, to put the matter into modal logic, the requirement is that $(x)\square(Fx \equiv Gx)$. Thus formulated, the requirement for identity of attributes is the same as the requirement for the identity of classes, but with the necessity operator inserted. For my part, however, I find this sort of account unsatisfactory because of my doubts over the notion of analyticity—to say nothing of modal logic.

Propositions are of course on a par with attributes. Two closed sentences are said to express the same proposition when they entail each other; when their biconditional is analytic, or holds necessarily. And I find the account similarly unsatisfactory.

I have contrasted classes with attributes in point of individuation. But I must stress that this is their only contrast. I must stress this fact because I have lately come to appreciate, to my surprise, that an old tendency still persists among philosophers to regard classes and attributes as radically unlike. It persists as an unarticulated feeling. I have been unable to elicit clear theses on the point, but I think I have sensed the association of ideas.

There seems to be an unarticulated feeling that a class is best given by enumeration. For large classes this is impossible, granted; but still it is felt that you know a class only insofar as you know its members. But may we not say equally that you know an attribute only insofar as you know what things have it? Well, the two cases are felt to differ. One cause of this feeling is perhaps an unconscious misreading of the principle that a class is "determined" by its members: as if to say that to find the class you must find its members. All it really means for classes to be determined by their members is that classes are the same that have the same members.

There seems, moreover, to be an unarticulated feeling that a class of widely dispersed objects is itself widely extended in the world, unwieldy, and hard to envisage. One cause of this feeling is perhaps an unconscious misreading of 'extension' or 'extensional'. The feeling is encouraged, and also evinced, by the use of such words as 'aggregate' to explain the notion of class, as if classes were concrete heaps or swarms. Indeed, the word 'class' itself, as if to say a fleet of ships, originated in this attitude. Likewise the word 'set'.

In contrast to all this, there is no reluctance to recognize that an attribute is normally specified by presenting an open sentence or predicate. The readiness to recognize this for attributes, despite not recognizing it for classes, is due perhaps to an unconscious tendency to confuse attributes with locutions, predicates. Indeed 'predicate' has notoriously been used in both senses, as was 'propositional function'. Attributes are thus associated with sentential conditions, while classes are associated with rosters or with heaps and swarms.

I am driven thus to psychological speculation as my only means of combatting the false contrast of class and attribute, because this misconception does not stand forth as an explicit thesis to refute. It is a serious misconception still, for it leads some philosophers to prefer attributes to classes, as somehow clear or more natural, even when they do not propose to distinguish between coextensive attributes. Let us recognize rather that if we are always to count coextensive attributes as identical, attributes *are* classes. Let us recognize that classes, like attributes, are abstract and immaterial, and that classes, like attributes, are epiphrastic. You specify a class not by its members but by its membership condition, its open sentence. Any proper reason to prefer attributes to classes must hinge only on distinctions between coextensive attributes.

Such distinctions are indeed present and called for in modal logic. Also, as we saw, the acceptance of modal logic carries with it the acceptance of a way of individuating attributes. Anyone who rejects this way of individuating attributes also rejects modal logic, as I do. Now it may be supposed that the only use of attributes is in model logic. If this supposition is true, there is no individuation problem for attributes; either we accept the individuation given by modal logic or we reject modal logic and so have no need of attributes. However, this supposition is uncertain; there may be a call for attributes independent of modal logic. Perhaps they are wanted in a theory of causality. In this event the problem of the individuation of attributes remains with us.

In an essay of 1958 called "Speaking of Objects,"[2] I raised the question whether we might just acquiesce in the faulty individuation of attributes and propositions by treating them as twilight entities, only real enough to be talked of in a few limited contexts, excluding the identity context. The plan is rather reminiscent of Frege on propositional functions. For his propositional functions may well be seen as attributes, and he accorded them only a shadowy existence: they were *ungesättigt*. It is a question of moderating the maxim "No entity without identity" to allow half-entity without identity. I raised the question in passing and remarked only that such a course would require some refashioning of logic. I propose now to explore the matter a bit further.

If we continue to speak of attributes as members of classes,

2. Reprinted in *Ontological Relativity*, pp. 1–25.

then we cannot dodge the question of identity of attributes. For given this much, we can coherently ask whether attributes A and B belong to all the same classes, and to ask this is to ask whether they are identical, even failing any *satisfactory* principle of individuation. If, therefore, we are to waive individuation for attributes, we must disallow class membership on the part of attributes.

In set theory, then, we find a possible candidate for the office of attribute, namely, *ultimate classes*. The phrase is mine, but the notion goes back to von Neumann, 1925. Some historians claim to find it already in Julius König, 1905, and even in Cantor, 1899; but this hinges on a question of interpretation.[3] Anyway, an ultimate class is a class that does not belong to any classes. In *Mathematical Logic* I called them nonelements. Often in the literature they are called proper classes. This perverse terminology has its etiology: they are classes *proper* as opposed to sets. But it *is* perverse; 'ultimate' is more suggestive.

The admitting of ultimate classes is one of the various ways of avoiding the antinomies of set theory, such as Russell's paradox. In the face of ultimate classes we can no longer ask, with Russell, about the class of all those classes that are not members of themselves. Since ultimate classes are members of none, the nearest we can come to Russell's paradoxical class is the class of all those *sets*, or nonultimate classes, that are not members of themselves. This is an ultimate class, and not a member of itself, and there is no contradiction.

Such was the purpose of ultimate classes. Russell avoided the antinomies by means rather of his theory of types, of course, and did not have the notion of an ultimate class. Still this notion induces, retroactively, some nostalgic reverberations also in Russell's writings. Away back in *Principles of Mathematics* Russell was exercised over the class as many and the class as one. The ultimate class, had he seen it, he might have seen as a class that existed only as many and not as one. Or, again, recall Russell's introduction to the second edition of Whitehead and Russell's *Principia Mathematica*.

---

3. See my *Set Theory and Its Logic*, p. 302.

There, influenced by Wittgenstein's *Tractatus*, Russell entertained the maxim that "a propositional function occurs only through its values." This echoes Frege on the *ungesättigt*. It is not clear how to make a coherent general doctrine of this maxim, without giving up general set theory. But the maxim does nicely fit the notion of an ultimate class. Being capable only of having members and not of being members, ultimate classes may be likened to propositional functions that occur only through their values.

Ultimate classes had as their purpose the avoidance of the antinomies, but perhaps we can now put them to another purpose: to serve as attributes. Ultimate classes are incapable of being members, and so are not captured by identity as Russell defines it; and identity conditions were all that stood between class and attribute. Reviving Russell's phrases, we can say that an attribute is a class as many, while a set is a class as one. An attribute is a propositional function that occurs only through its values.

Russell's definition of identity, however, now needs reconsideration. Membership on the part of ultimate classes has not been degrammaticized; it is merely denied. Hence Russell's definition of identity *can* be applied to ultimate classes, and it gives an absurd result: ultimate classes are all members of exactly the same classes, namely none, and are hence all identical—despite differing in their members. But here we are merely faced with the known and obvious fact that that definition of identity does not work for theories that admit objects belonging to no classes.

There *is* a way of constructing a suitable definition of identity within *any* theory, even a theory in which there is no talk of class and member at all. It is the method of exhaustion of the lexicon of predicates. A trivial example will remind you of how it runs. Suppose we have just two primitive one-place predicates '*F*' and '*G*', and one two-place predicate '*H*', and no constant singular terms or functors; just quantifiers and truth functions. Then we can define '$x = y$' as

$$Fx \equiv Fy \,.\, Gx \equiv Gy \,.\, (z)(Hxz \equiv Hyz \,.\, Hzx \equiv Hzy),$$

thus providing substitutivity in atomic contexts. The full logic of identity can be derived. The method obviously extends to any finite lexicon of primitive predicates, and it defines, every time, genuine identity or an indistinguishable facsimile: indistinguishable within the terms of the theory concerned.

We have just now run a curious course. In order to shield attributes from the identity question, we tried to shield them from membership in classes, such being Russell's definition of identity. But in so doing, and thus likening attributes to ultimate classes, we have disqualified Russell's definition of identity and thus nullified our motivation.

In conclusion let us briefly consider, then, how attributes must fare under our generalized approach to identity by exhaustion of predicates. Let us vaguely assume a rich, all-purpose lexicon of predicates, no mere trio of predicates as in the last example. Certain of these predicates will be desirable in application to attributes. One such is the two-place predicate 'has'; we want to be able to speak of an object as having an attribute. Many other predicates will be useless in application to attributes; thus it would be false, at best, to affirm, and useless, at best, to deny, that an attribute is pink or divisible by four. Ryle branded such predications category mistakes; he declared them meaningless and so did Russell in his theory of types. So did Carnap.

Over the years I have represented a minority of philosophers who preferred the opposite line: we can simplify grammar and logic by minimizing the number of our grammatical categories and maximizing their size. Instead of agreeing with Carnap that it is meaningless to say 'This stone is thinking about Vienna', and with Russell that it is meaningless to say 'Quadruplicity drinks procrastination', we can accommodate these sentences as meaningful and trivially false. Stones simply never think, as it happens, and quadruplicity never drinks.

For our present inquiry into attributes, however, we are bound to take rather the line of Ryle, Russell, and Carnap. We must separate the serious predications from the silly ones. We must think in terms of a many-sorted logic with many sorts of variables, some of which are grammatically attachable to some predicates and some to others. Then we can look to that partial lexicon of just those predicates that are attachable to attribute variables and to attribute names; and we can proceed to define identity of attributes by exhaustion of just those predicates. If we keep those predicates to just the ones that may seriously and usefully be affirmed of attributes, and denied of attributes, then the identity relation defined by exhaustion of those predicates should be just right for attributes.

Stated less cumbersomely, what we are seeking as an identity relation of attributes is a relation which assures interchangeability, *salva veritate,* in all contexts that are worthwhile for attribute variables. Let us try, then, to name a few such contexts. One conspicuous one we have named is the context 'has'. On the other hand, a context that is still unwelcome, presumably, is the membership context: we do not want to recognize the question of membership of attributes in classes. For if membership of attributes in classes were accepted, we could again apply Russell's shortcut definition of identity, and so again we would have identity of attributes without any instructive principle of individuation. For that matter, even the 'has' context is presumably welcome only when the mention of attributes is restricted to the righthand side; for we do not want to recognize attributes of attributes. If we recognized them, we could say that attributes are identical when they have all the same attributes, and so again we would have identity of attributes without any instructive principle of individuation. For the same reason, of course, a primitive predicate of identity would be an unwelcome context for attribute variables; and so would contexts where attributes are counted. Thus we should be prepared, at least until solving our identity problem, to abstain from saying that Napoleon had all the attributes of a great general save one—though remaining free to say that Napoleon had all the attributes of a great general.

This last example, of course, mentions attributes only in the same old 'has' context. *Are* there other desirable contexts, or are all desirable contexts of attribute variables parasitic on 'has' and reducible to it by paraphrase?

In the latter event, our definition of identity of attributes by exhaustion of lexicon is the work of a moment. The relevant lexicon is meager indeed, having 'has' as its only member; and thus attributes come out identical if exactly the same things *have* them. In this event, attributes are extensional; we might as well read 'has' as membership, and call attributes classes; but they are classes as many, not as one, for we are declaring it ungrammatical to represent them as members of further classes. They occur only through their values. They are ultimate classes, except that now we do not deny their membership in other classes; we degrammaticize it. Some set-theorists, Bernays among them,[4] have already taken this line with ultimate classes too.

If on the other hand there are desirable contexts of attribute variables that do not reduce to 'has', then let us have a list of them in the form of a list of appropriate primitive predicates of attributes. Given the list, we know how to define identity of attributes in terms of it. It should be possible to produce the list, and thus to individuate attributes, if attributes really serve any good purpose not served by classes.

4. See my *Set Theory and Its Logic*, p. 313. On identifying attributes with ultimate classes see Geach, *Logic Matters*, p. 233.

13

Intensions Revisited

For the necessity predicate, as distinct from the necessity functor '□', I shall write 'Nec'. I affirm it of a sentence, to mean that the sentences is a necessary truth, or, if one like, analytic. Whatever its shortcomings in respect of clear criteria, the predicate is more comfortable than the sentence functor, for it occasions no departure from extensional logic. Hence there would be comfort in being able to regard '□' as mere shorthand for 'Nec' and a pair of quotation marks—thus '□(9 is odd)' for 'Nec '9 is odd' '. But it will not do. In modal logic one wants to quantify into necessity contexts, and we cannot quantify into quotations.

We can adjust matters by giving 'Nec' *multigrade* status :[1] letting it figure as an n-place predicate for each n. As a two-place predicate it amounts to the words 'is necessarily true of'; thus Nec('odd', 9). As a three-place predicate it amounts to those same words said of a two-place predicate and two objects; thus Nec('<', 5, 9). And so on up. In terms now of multigrade 'Nec' we can explain the use of '□' on open sentences. We can explain '□(x is odd)', '□($x < y$)', etc., as short for 'Nec('odd', x)', 'Nec ('<', x, y)', etc.[2] There is no longer an obstacle to quantifying into '□(x is odd)', '□($x < y$)', etc. since the definientia do not quote the variables.

Reprinted from *Midwest Studies in Philosophy* 2 (1977).

1. The word was first used by Goodman, at my suggestion.
2. Kaplan anticipated this procedure in his third footnote.

This multigrade use of 'Nec' is much like my multigrade treatment in 1956 of the verbs of propositional attitude.[3] Critics of that paper reveal that I have to explain—what I thought went without saying—that the adoption of a multi-grade predicate involves no logical anomaly or any infinite lexicon. It can be viewed as a one-place predicate whose arguments are sequences. As for the use of quotation, it of course is reducible by inductive definition to the concatenation functor and names of signs.

Perhaps also a caution is in order regarding two ways of taking 'necessarily true'. The sentence '9 is odd' is a necessary truth; still, that the form of words '9 is odd' means what it does, and is thus true at all, is only a contingent fact of social usage. Of course I intend 'Nec' in the former way. Similarly for its polyadic use, applied to predicates.

Commonly the predicate wanted as argument of 'Nec' will not be available in the language as a separate word or consecutive phrase. At that point the 'such that' functor serves. For example, the definiens of '$\Box((x + y)(x - y) = x^2 - y^2)$' is:

$$\text{Nec}('zw \; 3 \, ((z + w)(z - w) = z^2 - w^2)', x, y).$$

The 'such that' functor, 'zw 3' in this example, connotes no abstraction of classes or relations or attributes. It is only a device for forming complex predicates, tantamount to relative clauses.[4]

When predication in the mode of necessity is directed upon a variable, the necessity is *de re*: the predicate is meant to be true of the value of the variable by whatever name, there being indeed no name at hand. 'Nec('odd',x)' says of the unspecified object x that oddity is of its essence. Thus it is true not only that Nec('odd', 9), but equally that Nec('odd', number of planets), since this very object 9, essence and all, happens to *be* the number of the planets. The 'Nec' notation accommodates *de dicto* necessity too, but differently: the term concerned *de dicto* is within the quoted sentence or predicate. Thus 'Nec '9 is odd' ', unlike 'Nec('odd', 9)', is *de*

---

3. "Quantifiers and propositional attitudes," reprinted in *Ways of Paradox*.

4. See Essay 1 above, §I.

dicto, and 'Nec 'number of planets is odd' ', unlike 'Nec ('odd', number of planets)', is false.

De re and *de dicto* can be distinguished also in terms of '$\Box$', but along other lines. When the term concerned is a variable, there is nothing to distinguish; *de re* is *de rigueur.* When it is not a variable, we keep it in the scope of '$\Box$' for *de dicto*:

$$\Box \text{(number of planets is odd)} \qquad \text{(false)}$$

and bring it out thus for *de re*:

(1) $(\exists x)(x = \text{number of planets.} \Box (x \text{ is odd}))$.   (true)

In the system of definitions of '$\Box$' in terms of 'Nec' we observe a radical twist: '$\Box (x$ is odd)' and '$\Box$ (number of planets is odd)' look alike in form, as do 'Nec ('odd', x)' and 'Nec ('odd', number of planets)', but the translations do not run true to form. '$\Box (x$ is odd)' and '$\Box$ (number of planets is odd)' stand rather for the dissimilar formulas 'Nec ('odd', x)' and 'Nec 'number of planets is odd' ', whereas what stands for 'Nec ('odd', number of planets)' is (1).

Definitional expansion of '$\Box$' thus goes awry under substitution of constants for variables. This is legitimate; unique eliminability is the only formal demand on definition. What the irregularity does portend is a drastic difference in form between the modal logic of '$\Box$' and such laws as govern its defining predicate 'Nec'. Drastic difference there is indeed. In particular the distinction between *de re* and *de dicto* is drawn with a simpler uniformity in terms of 'Nec' than in terms of '$\Box$'.

Some simplification of theory can be gained by dispensing with singular terms other than variables in familiar fashion: primitive names can be dropped in favor of uniquely fulfilled predicates and then restored as singular descriptions, which finally can be defined away in essentially Russell's way. That done, we can explain '$\Box$' fully in terms of 'Nec' and vice versa by this schematic biconditional :

(2) $\Box F x_1 x_2 \ldots x_n \equiv \text{Nec} ('F', x_1, x_2, \ldots, x_n)$.

Here n may be 0. A certain liberty has been taken in quoting a schematic letter.

It may be noted in passing that '$\Box$' on the left of (2) could alternatively be viewed not as a sentence functor but as a predicate functor, governing just the 'F' and forming a modal predicate '$\Box F$'.[5]

The reconstruction of '$\Box$' in terms of 'Nec' has lent some clarity to the foundations of modal logic by embedding it in extensional logic, quotation, and a special predicate. Incidentally the contrast between *de re* and *de dicto* has thereby been heightened. But the special predicate takes some swallowing. In its monadic use it is at best the controversial semantic predicate of analyticity, and in its polyadic use it imposes an essentialist metaphysics. Let me be read, then, as expounding rather than propounding. I am in the position of a Jewish chef preparing ham for a gentile clientele. Analyticity, essence, and modality are not my meat.

If these somber reflections make one wonder whether 'Nec' may be more than we need for '$\Box$', a negative answer is visible in (2) : they are interdefinable.[5a]

A project that I shall not undertake is that of codifying laws of 'Nec' from which those of modal logic can be derived through the definitions. The laws of 'Nec' would involve continual interplay between quotations and their contents. Obviously we would want:

$$\text{Nec '}\ldots\text{'} \supset \ldots,$$

where the dots stand for any closed sentence. Also, where '——' and '. . .' stand for any closed sentences, we would want 'Nec '—— ≡ . . .'' to assure the interchangeability of '——' with '. . .' inside any quotation preceded by 'Nec'. This is needed for the substitutivity of '$\Box$(—— ≡ . . .)' in the modal logic. Also we would need corresponding laws governing the polyadic use of 'Nec' in application to predicates; and here complexities mount. No doubt modal logic is better codified in its own terms; such is the very utility of defining '$\Box$' instead of staying with 'Nec'. The latter is merely of conceptual interest in distilling the net import of modal logic over and above extensional logic.

Necessity *de dicto* is notoriously resistant to the substitu-

---

5. For the truth theory of a functor to this effect see Peacocke.
5a. But see Schilpp and Hahn (eds.), pp. 269, 279 (n. 27), 293.

tivity of identity. When only variables are concerned, the question does not arise; for they figure only *de re,* or, as I have often put it, only in referential position. Moreover, we have decided that only variables *are* concerned, definitions aside. Still, let us consider how singular terms fare when restored definitionally as descriptions. Expanded by those definitions, an identity joining two descriptions or a description and a variable obviously implies the corresponding universally quantified biconditional. We may be sure therefore that even in *de dicto* positions, where substitutivity of simple identity fails, we can depend on substitutivity of necessary identity, $\Box(\zeta = \eta)$; this is assured by the substitutivity of '$\Box(\underline{\quad} \equiv \dots)$' noted above.

The substitutivity of $\ulcorner\Box(\zeta = \eta)\urcorner$ is gospel in modal logic. Still, some readers are perhaps brought up short by my appeal to $\ulcorner\Box(\zeta = \eta)\urcorner$, as if I did not know that

(3) $(x)(y)(x = y \,.\, \supset \Box(x = \mathrm{y}))$.

The point is that I am not free to put ζ and η for '*x*' and '*y*' in (3). Instantiation of quantifications by singular terms is under the same wraps as the substitutivity of identity.

Let instantiation then be our next topic. From the true universal quantification:

$(x)(x$ is a number $.\supset.\,\Box(5 < x) \vee \Box(5 \geqq x))$

we cannot, one hopes, infer the falsehood:

$\Box(5 <$ number of planets$) \vee \Box(5 \geqq$ number of planets$)$.

From the truth:

$5 <$ number of planets $.\,-\Box(5 <$ number of planets$)$,

again, we cannot, one hopes, infer the falsehood:

$(\exists x)(5 < x \,.\, -\Box(5 < x))$.

When *can* we trust the instantial laws of quantification? The answer is implicit in the substitutivity of $\ulcorner\Box(\zeta = \eta)\urcorner$. For, instantiation is unquestioned when the instantial term is a mere variable '*x*'; and we can supplant '*x*' here by any desired term η, thanks to the substitutivity of $\ulcorner\Box(x = \eta)\urcorner$, if we can establish $\ulcorner(\exists x)\Box(x = \eta)\urcorner$. This last, then, is the condition that qualifies a term η for the instantial role in steps of universal instantiation and existential generalization in modal contexts. A term thus qualified is what Føllesdal called a genuine name and Kripke has called a rigid designator.[6] It is a term such that $(\exists x)\square(x = a)$, that is, something is necessarily a, where 'a' stands for the term.

Such a term enjoys *de re* privileges even in a *de dicto* setting. Besides acquitting themselves in instantiation, such terms lend themselves in pairs to the substitutivity of simple identity. For, where ζ and η are rigid designators, we are free to put them for 'x' and 'y' in (3) and thus derive necessary identity.

A rigid designator differs from others in that it picks out its object by essential traits. It designates the object in all possible worlds in which it exists. Talk of possible worlds is a graphic way of waging the essentialist philosophy, but it is only that; it is not an explication. Essence is needed to identify an object from one possible world to another.

Let us turn now to the propositional attitudes. As remarked above, my treatment of them in 1956 resembled my present use of 'Nec'. At that time I provisionally invoked attributes and propositions, however reluctantly, for the roles here played by mere predicates and sentences. Switching now to the latter style, I would write:

(4) Tom believes 'Cicero denounced Catiline',

(5) Tom believes 'x ϶ (x denounced Catiline)' of Cicero,

(6) Tom believes 'x ϶ (Cicero denounced x)' of Catiline,

(7) Tom believes 'xy ϶ (x denounced y)' of Cicero, Catiline,

depending on which terms I want in referential position—that is, with respect to which terms I want the belief to be *de re*. The multigrade predicate 'believes' in these examples is dyadic, triadic, triadic, and tetradic.

Whatever the obscurities of the notion of belief, the underlying logic thus far is extensional—as in the case of 'Nec'. But we can immediately convert the whole to an intensional logic of belief, analogous to that of '$\square$'. Where 'B_t'

6. Kripke, see below, p. 173.

is a sentence functor ascribing belief to Tom, the analogue of the sketchy translation schema (2) is this:

$B_t F x_1 x_2 \ldots x_n \equiv.$ Tom believes 'F' of $x_1, x_2, \ldots, x_n$.

Parallel to (1) we get:

$(\exists x)(x = \text{Cicero} \,.\, B_t(x \text{ denounced Catiline}))$,

$(\exists x)(x = \text{Catiline} \,.\, B_t(\text{Cicero denounced } x))$,

$(\exists x)(\exists y)(x = \text{Cicero} \,.\, y = \text{Catiline} \,.\, B_t(x \text{ denounced } y))$

as our transcriptions of the *de re* constructions (5)–(7).

In the 1956 paper I dwelt on the practical difference between the *de dicto* statement:

(8)   Ralph believes '$(\exists x)(x$ is a spy)'

and the *de re* statement 'There is someone whom Ralph believes to be a spy', that is:

(9) $(\exists y)$ (Ralph believes 'spy' of y).

I noted also the more narrowly logical difference between the *de dicto* statement:

(10)   Ralph believes 'Ortcutt is a spy'

and the *de re* statement:

(11)   Ralph believes 'spy' of Ortcutt,

and conjectured that the step of 'exportation' leading from (10) to (11) is generally valid. However, if we transcribe (10) and (11) into terms of 'B_r' according to the foregoing patterns, we get:

(12) B_r (Ortcutt is a spy),

(13) $(\exists x)(x = \text{Ortcutt} \,.\, B_r(x \text{ is a spy}))$,

and here the existential force of (13) would seem to belie the validity of the exportation. Sleigh, moreover, has challenged this step on other grounds. Surely, he observes (nearly enough), Ralph believes there are spies. If he believes further, as he reasonably may, that

(14)   No two spies are of exactly the same height,

then he will believe that the shortest spy is a spy. If exportation were valid, it would follow that

> Ralph believes 'spy' of the shortest spy,

and this, having the term 'the shortest spy' out in referential position, implies (9). Thus the portentous belief (9) would follow from trivial ones, (8) and belief of (14).

Let us consult incidentally the analogues of (10) and (11) in modal logic. Looking to the transcriptions (12) and (13), we see that the analogous modal structures are '$\Box Fa$' and '$(\exists x)(x = a . \Box Fx)$'. Does the one imply the other? Again the existential force of the latter would suggest not. And again we can dispute the implication also apart from that existential consideration, as follows [abbreviating (14) and 'there are spies' in conjunction as '14'] :

(15) $\Box(14 \supset$. the shortest spy is a spy),

(16) $(\exists x)(x = $ the shortest spy . $\Box(14 \supset . x$ is a spy$))$.

Surely (15) is true. On the other hand, granted (14), presumably (16) is false; for it would require someone to be a spy *de re*, or in essence.

Evidently we must find against exportation. Kaplan's judgment, which he credits to Montgomery Furth, is that the step is sound only in the case of what he calls a *vivid* designator, which is the analogue, in the logic of belief, of a rigid designator. And what might this analogue be? We saw that in modal logic a term is a rigid designator if $(\exists x)\Box(x = a)$, where 'a' stands for the term; so the parallel condition for the logic of belief is that $(\exists x)B_t(x = a)$, if Tom is our man. Thus a term is a vivid designator, for Tom, when there is a specific thing that he believes it designates. Vivid designators, analogues of the rigid designators in modal logic, are the terms that can be freely used to instantiate quantifications in belief contexts, and that are subject to the substitutivity of identity—and, now, to exportation.

Hintikka's criterion for this superior type of term was that Tom *know* who or what the person or thing is; whom or what the term designates.[7] The difference is accountable to

7. Hintikka, *Knowledge and Belief*.

the fact that Hintikka's was a logic of both belief and knowledge.

The notion of knowing or believing who or what someone or something is, is utterly dependent on context. Sometimes, when we ask who someone is, we see the face and want the name; sometimes the reverse. Sometimes we want to know his role in the community.[8] Of itself the notion is empty.

It and the notion of essence are on a par. Both make sense in context. Relative to a particular inquiry, some predicates may play a more basic role than others, or may apply more fixedly; and these may be treated as essential. The respective derivative notions, then, of vivid designator and rigid designator, are similarly dependent on context and empty otherwise. The same is true of the whole quantified modal logic of necessity; for it collapses if essence is withdrawn. For that matter, the very notion of necessity makes sense to me only relative to context. Typically it is applied to what is assumed in an inquiry, as against what has yet to transpire.

In thus writing off modal logic I find little to regret. Regarding the propositional attitudes, however, I cannot be so cavalier. Where does the passing of the vivid designator leave us with respect to belief? It leaves us with no distinction between admissible and inadmissible cases of the exportation that leads from (10) to (11), except that those cases remain inadmissible in which the exported term fails to name anything. It leaves us defenseless against Sleigh's deduction of the strong (9) from (8) and belief of (14). Thus it virtually annuls the seemingly vital contrast between (8) and (9) : between merely believing there are spies and suspecting a specific person. At first this seems intolerable, but it grows on one. I now think the distinction is every bit as empty, apart from context, as that of vivid designator: that of knowing or believing who someone is. In context it can still be important. In one case we can be of service by pointing out the suspect; in another, by naming him; in others, by giving his address or specifying his ostensible employment.

Renunciation does not stop here. The condition for being

8. Such variation is recognized by Hintikka, *Knowledge and Belief*, p. 149n. For a study of it in depth see Boër and Lycan.

a vivid designator is that $(\exists x) B_t (x = a)$, or, in the other notation, that

$$(\exists x) \; (\text{Tom believes } 'y \; 3 \; (y = a)' \text{ of } x).$$

Surely this makes every bit as good sense as the idiom 'believes of'; there can be no trouble over $'y \; 3 \; (y = a)'$. So our renunciation must extend to all *de re* belief, and similarly, no doubt, for the other propositional attitudes. We end up rejecting *de re* or quantified propositional attitudes generally, on a par with *de re* or quantified modal logic. Rejecting them, that is, except as idioms relativized to the context or situation at hand. We remain less cavalier toward propositional attitudes than toward modal logic only in the unquantified or *de dicto* case, where the attitudes are taken as dyadic relations between people or other animals and closed sentences.

Even these relations present difficulties in respect of criterion. Belief is not to be recognized simply by assent, for this leaves no place for insincerity or sanctimonious self-deception. Belief can be nicely tested and even measured by the betting odds that the subject will accept, allowance being made for the positive or negative value for him of risk as such. This allowance can be measured by testing him on even chances. However, bets work only for sentences for which there is a verification or falsification procedure acceptable to both parties as settling the bet. I see the verb 'believe' even in its *de dicto* use as varying in meaningfulness from sentence to sentence.

Ascribed to the dumb and illiterate animal, belief *de dicto* seems a *contradictio in adjecto*. The betting test is never available. I have suggested elsewhere that some propositional attitudes—desire, fear—might be construed as a relation of the animal to a set of sets of his sensory receptors; but this works only for what I called egocentric desire and fear.[9] I see no way of extending this to belief. Certainly the ascription of a specific simple belief to a dumb animal often can be supported by citing its observable behavior; but a general definition to the purpose is not evident.

---

9. "Propositional objects," reprinted in *Ontological Relativity*.

Raymond Nelson has ascribed beliefs to machines. He has done so in support of a mechanist philosophy, and I share his attitude. The objects of belief with which he deals are discrete, observable alternatives, and the machine's belief or expectation with respect to them lends itself to a straightforward definition. But this is of no evident help in the kind of problem that is exercising me here. For my problem is not one of reconciling mind and matter, but only a quest for general criteria suitable for unprefabricated cases.

14

Worlds Away

Identifying an object from world to possible world is analogous, it has been suggested,[1] to identifying an object from moment to moment in our world. I agree, and I want now to develop the analogy.

Consider my broad conception of a physical object: the material content of any portion of space-time, however scattered and discontinuous. Equivalently: any sum or aggregate of point-events. The world's water is for me a physical object, comprising all the molecules of H_2O anywhere ever. There is a physical object part of which is a momentary stage of a silver dollar now in my pocket and the rest of which is a temporal segment of the Eiffel Tower through its third decade. I am using 'there is' tenselessly (Sellars: 'there be').

Any two momentary objects, then, taken at different moments, are time slices of some one time-extended physical object; time slices, indeed, of each of many such. Thus consider the present momentary stage of that sliver dollar in my otherwise empty pocket; and consider a momentary stage of that same coin next Tuesday, again in my otherwise empty pocket. One object of which these two momentary objects are time slices is the coin. Another object of which they are

Reprinted from the *Journal of Philosophy* 73 (1976). Two of the paragraphs near the end have been dropped because of coverage in the preceding essay.

1. E.g., by Hintikka, *Intentions of Intentionality*, ch. 6.

time slices is the monetary content of my pocket—a discontinuous object that has had some nickel and copper content along the way. A third and more inclusive object of which they are time slices is the total content of my pocket, there being intrusive stages of a key or pillbox. Identification of an object from moment to moment is indeed on a par with identifying an object from world to world : both identifications are vacuous, pending further directives.

Identification of an object from moment to moment takes on content only when we indicate what sort of object we want.[2] The two momentary objects last studied are indeed time slices of *the* same *coin*. If for my convenience my friendly neighborhood banker changes the coin to quarters, then the earlier time slice of my coin and a later scattered time slice of my four coins may be said to be time slices of *the* same *dollar*, in one sense of the word.

Among the myriad ways, mostly uninteresting, of stacking up momentary objects to make time-extended objects, there is one popular favorite : the corporeal. Momentary objects are declared to be stages of the same body by considerations of continuity of displacement, continuity of deformation, continuity of chemical change. These are not conditions on the notion of identity; they are conditions on the notion of body. Most of our common predicates, like 'coin', denote only bodies, and so derive their individuation from the individuation of the predicate 'body'; and individuation is nine parts cross-moment identification. 'Dollar' was a rather labored exception to the bodily mode of integration, and of course countless still more artificial examples can be devised.

Despite men's stubborn body-mindedness, there are good reason for the more liberal ontology of physical objects.[3] All these objects, when I quantify over individuals, are the

2. My point is strangely reminiscent of Geach's contention that "it makes no sense to judge whether x and y are 'the same' . . . unless we add or understand some genral term—'the same F'" (§31). I say "strangely" because I disagree with Geach; I insist that x and y are the same F if and only if x and y are the same, outright, and Fx. Cross-moment identification is another thing; the momentary objects x and y are unwaveringly distinct, but are time slices of perhaps the same F and different G's. See Geach, *Reference and Generality*.

3. See Essay 1 above, §II.

values of my variables. And what, then, would be the analogous values of variables if one were to quantify over individuals in all possible worlds? Simply the sums of physical objects of the various worlds, combining denizens of different worlds indiscriminately. One of these values would consist of Napoleon together with his counterparts in other worlds, if 'counterpart' made sense; another would consist of Napoleon together with sundry utterly dissimilar denizens of other worlds.

Thus quantification over objects across possible worlds does not require us to make any sense of 'counterpart'. Just as any two momentary objects in different moments are shared as time slices not by just one time-extended object but by countless ones, so any two physical objects in different worlds are shared as realizations not by just one intermundane object but by countless ones. Quantification is as straightforward over the one domain as over the other, unless there is some independent trouble with possible worlds.

And indeed there is. It lies elsewhere: not in the quantification, but in the predicates. We saw that in our own world the identification of a physical object from moment to moment makes sense only relative to the principle of individuation of one or another particular predicate—usually, though not necessarily, the predicate 'body' or one of its subordinates. Such cross-moment groupings are indifferent to the actual quantification over physical objects, since the quantification respects all cross-moment groups, however random. But they matter to the predicates. If a sentence begins '(x) (x is a coin .$\supset$', the physical objects that are going to matter as values of its variable are just the coins; and thus the way of identifying a coin from moment to moment can be relevant to the truth value of the sentence. Since all sentences contain predicates, cross-moment identification of one sort or another is a crucial matter in its proper place.

Similarly, if one quantifies over objects across possible worlds, one needs cross-world identification relative to whatever predicates one uses in such sentences. Typically these predicates, again, will be subordinates of 'body'. Insofar, then, we could accommodate them if we could somehow extend our principle of individuation or integration of bodies so as to identify bodies not just from moment to moment, as we do so well, but from world to world. However, our cross-moment identification of bodies turned on continuity of displacement, distortion, and chemical change. These considerations cannot be extended across the worlds, because you can change anything to anything by easy stages through some connecting series of possible worlds. The devastating difference is that the series of momentary cross sections of our real world is uniquely imposed on us, for better or for worse, whereas all manner of paths of continuous gradation from one possible world to another are free for the thinking up.

To see how quantification into modal contexts depends on cross-world identifications, or counterparts, consider '$(\exists x) \Box Fx$'. The problem is not in the quantification as such, as we saw; 'x' ranges over all manner of ill-assorted cross-world hybrids. 'Fx', however, stands for some sentence built up of 'x' and various predicates and logical constants. Or we may as well think of 'F' itself as a predicate, primitive or defined. The quantification '$(\exists x) \Box Fx$' says that among the objects fulfilling 'F' in our world there is some one (among perhaps many) all of whose counterparts in other possible worlds fulfill 'F'. For this to make sense, we need to make cross-world sense not of 'same object', which is vacuous, but of 'same F'. We need cross-world individuation of the predicate 'F'. Or nearly so. We could manage with a little less. Cross-world individuation of some predicate subordinate to 'F' would suffice if that predicate happened to be fulfilled by one of the objects whose counterparts are all supposed to fulfill 'F'. Here, indeed, is a strategy that can be pressed to advantage: pick the narrowest predicate you can, so long as you can count on it to catch one of the objects whose counterparts are all supposed to fulfill 'F'. For, the narrower it is, the fewer the objects are for which we need to specify counterparts, or cross-world identities. The limit of this strategy, if it can be managed, is a uniquely fulfilled predicate, true of just a single object whose counterparts are all supposed to fulfill 'F'; for then there is just the one object demanding definition of cross-world identity.

Imagine a case where this has been managed. It is asserted that $(\exists x) \Box Fx$, and this is supported by producing a predicate '*G*' that is purportedly fulfilled uniquely by an x such that $\square \, Fx$. All that then needs to be done to make sense of all this, if not to prove it, is to cite conditions of cross-world identity for the object x such that Gx. But the analogy of identification over time is still of no help.

Instead of bandying a uniquely fulfilled predicate '*G*', one may forge a corresponding singular term '*g*'. Here, then, is the rigid designator.[4]

Hintikka has explained that he is not a champion of alethic modal logic, the logic of necessity. But he is very much a champion, in two senses, of the modal logic of propositional attitudes. He urges that things are different there. Paths of continuous gradation from one belief world to another are not free for the thinking up. The belief worlds coincide with one another in all details in which the believer believes, and at other points they are still pretty well behaved, being compatible with his beliefs. In large part it does make sense to identify a body from one such world to another.

Yes, but not always. Each belief world will include countless bodies that are not separately recognizable objects of the believer's beliefs at all, for the believer does believe still that there are countless such bodies. Questions of identity of these, from world to world, remain as devoid of sense as they were in the possible worlds of alethic modal logic. Yet how are they to be dismissed, if one is to quantify into belief contexts? Perhaps the values of such variables should be limited to objects that the believer has pretty detailed views about. How detailed? I do not see the makings here of a proper annex to austere scientific language.

4. See the preceding essay.

15

Grades of Discriminability

An object may be said to be *specifiable,* in a given interpreted formal language, if in that language there is an open sentence, in one free variable, that is uniquely satisfied by that object. Two objects are *discriminable* if there is an open sentence, in one free variable, that is satisfied by one of the objects and not the other. Objects may be discriminable without being specifiable. It is well known that not all real numbers are specifiable; yet all are discriminable, as is evident from the fact that any two reals are separated by a ratio. For any two reals there are numerals μ and ν such that the open sentence $\ulcorner x < \mu/\nu \urcorner$ is satisfied by one of the reals and not by the other.

But discriminability does assure specifiability in the infinite, so to speak. If all the objects of a domain are discriminable, obviously each of them uniquely satisfies the infinite conjunction—better, the set—of all the open sentences in 'x' that it satisfies. Each real number is uniquely determined by the set of all the sentences $\ulcorner x < \mu/\nu \urcorner$ that it satisfies.

Discriminability, in the sense defined, will be referred to more particularly as *strong discriminability* to distinguish it from weaker grades to which I now turn. I shall call two objects *moderately discriminable* if there is an open sentence

Reprinted from the *Journal of Philosophy* 73 (1976).

in two free variables that is satisfied by the two objects in one
order and not in the other order. Objects can be discriminable
in this sense without being strongly discriminable. The
ordinal numbers afford an example. All ordinals are moderately discriminable, since any two of them satisfy the open
sentence '$x < y$' in one order and not the other. Yet they are
not all strongly discriminable. If they were, then, as remarked, each ordinal would be uniquely determined by the
set of the open sentences that it satisfies. Sentences, being
finite in length, are denumerable, so the number of sets of
sentences is the power of the continuum. Thus if the ordinals
were strongly discriminable they would be limited in number to the power of the continuum.

In treating of discriminability I am not assuming in general that the languages concerned contain the predicate '='.
In general, however, whether or not a language contains '=',
there is a familiar sense in which we can speak of the utter
indiscriminability of objects x and y in the language. It is
simply that

(1) $(z_1) (z_2) \ldots (z_n) (Fxz_1z_2 \ldots z_n \supset Fyz_1z_2 \ldots z_n)$

for all n and all open sentences of the language in the role of
'$Fxz_1z_2 \ldots z_n$'. Thus the weakest possible condition of discriminability of objects x and y is that there be an open sentence for the role of '$Fxz_1z_2 \ldots z_n$' such that, contrary to (1),

(2) $(\exists z_1) (\exists z_2) \ldots (\exists z_n) (Fxz_1z_2 \ldots z_n . - Fyz_1z_2 \ldots z_n)$.

But in fact this formulation is needlessly cumbersome. Its
purpose is already served by its simplest case, where $n = 0$:
the case '$Fx . - Fy$'. If objects x and y can be discriminated
by a sentence of the form (2) at all, they can already be discriminated by a sentence of the short form '$Fx . - Fy$'. For
(2) implies something of this short form. To see this, ab-
breviate (2) as 'G_yx'; then 'G_yy' is inconsistent; so (2) implies '$G_yx . - G_yy$'.

Here, then, is the definition of *weak discriminability*, the
weakest possible: satisfaction of a sentence of the form
'$Fx . - Fy$'. This definition looks equivalent to the definition
of strong discriminability; 'Fx' stands for an open sentence
that is satisfied, it would seem, by the one object and not the

other. Actually the definitions are far from equivalent; we shall find that weak discriminability is even weaker than moderate discriminability. The reason for failure of equivalence is that a sentence of the form '$Fx \, . - Fy$' can have 'x' and 'y' as sole free variables and yet not be the conjunction of two sentences that have 'x' and 'y' respectively as sole free variables. This can happen because of an extra occurrence of 'x' or 'y' hidden, so to speak, in the 'F'. It happened at the end of the preceding paragraph, where '$G_y x \, . - G_y y$' was recognized as a correct substitution instance of '$Fx \, . - Fy$'.

To show that weak discriminability differs not only from strong but also from moderate discriminability, I need a lemma regarding the logic of identity.

Lemma. If an open sentence is built up of just '$=$' and variables by quantification and truth functions, then in any infinite universe it is equivalent to a mere truth function of equations of its free variables. (Equivalent in the sense of agreeing in truth value for all values of the variables.)

Proof by elimination of quantifiers, as follows. Translate universal quantifications into existential, and then drive quantifiers inward by putting their scopes into alternational normal form, distributing the quantifiers through the alternations, and exporting any unbound components of conjunctions. Banish any self-identities by obvious reductions. Each innermost quantification is now of this sort:

$$(\exists z)\,(z = u_1 \, . \, z = u_2 \, . \, \ldots \, . \, z = u_m \, . \, z \neq v_1 \, . \, z \neq v_2 \, . \, \ldots \, . \, z \neq v_n)$$

But we can drop '$(\exists z)$' and '$z = u_1$' here, putting 'u_1' for 'z' in the further clauses (if any). Or if $m = 0$, we can mark the quantification true and resolve it out, since the infinitude of the universe assures that

$$(\exists z)\,(z \neq v_1 \, . \, z \neq v_2 \, . \, \ldots \, . \, z \neq v_n)$$

In this way each innermost quantifier disappears and no new free variables emerge.

To see now that weak discriminability is weaker than moderate, consider an interpreted language with '$=$' as sole predicate and an infinite universe. Any of its sentences whose free variables are 'x' and 'y' is equivalent, by the lemma, to a truth function of '$x = x$', '$y = y$', and '$x = y$', hence to '$x = y$' or '$x \neq y$' or 'T' or '$\bot$'. So none of its sentences in two free variables is satisfied by objects in one order and not the other. So none of its objects are moderately discriminable. Yet any two of its objects are weakly discriminable, satisfying as they do the sentence '$x = x$. $x \neq y$', which has the form 'Fx . $- Fy$'.

Ivan Fox has suggested to me another criterion of discriminability: that the objects satisfy some irreflexive sentence in two free variables. Since any sentence of the form 'Fx . $- Fy$' is irreflexive [i.e., $(z) - (Fz . - Fz)$], any objects that are weakly discriminable in my sense are discriminable in his. So, since my weak discriminability is minimal, his is equivalent. (Or, to argue this converse anew, let us represent his irreflexive sentence as 'H_yx'. Because of the irreflexivity, any two objects satisfying 'H_yx' satisfy 'H_yx . $- H_yy$', which has the form 'Fx . $- Fy$'.)

We can trim Fox's criterion a little by requiring not that his open sentence be irreflexive, but just that it be reflexively false of one of the objects to be discriminated. Clearly, the equivalence argument above is unimpeded by this emendation. Thus phrased, the criterion of weak discriminability is this: a sentence in two variables is satisfied by the two objects but not by one of them with itself. This version may be preferred to my earlier equivalent—viz., satisfaction of a sentence of the form 'Fx . $- Fy$'—on two counts: it calls for no consideration of hidden occurrences of 'x' and 'y', and it fits the style of the definitions of specification and strong and moderate discrimination. Let us see them together. A sentence in one variable *specifies* an object if satisfied by it uniquely. A sentence in one variable *strongly discriminates* two objects if satisfied by one and not the other. A sentence in two variables *moderately discriminates* two objects if satisfied by them in one order only. A sentence in two variables *weakly discriminates* two objects if satisfied by the two but not by one of them with itself.

But the earlier way of stating weak discriminability retains interest for its subtle contrast with strong discriminability: we had 'Fx . $- Fy$' on the one hand and 'Fx' and '$- Fy$' on the other. It is remarkable that there is yet another grade of discriminability between the two.

May there even be many intermediate grades? The question is ill defined. By imposing special conditions on the form or content of the open sentence used in discriminating two objects, we could define any number of intermediate grades of discriminability, subject even to no linear order. What I have called moderate discriminability, however, is the only intermediate grade that I see how to define at our present high level of generality.

16

Lewis Carroll's Logic

Lewis Carroll has meant much to most of us. Some of us do not outgrow him. There are playful absurdities in his tales that tickle the logical mind. Now and again a passage of his can be aptly quoted in the course of some philosophical analysis, and the quotation sensibly leavens the lump. A posthumous new book of his after lo these eighty years is an event not to be lightly passed over.

Curiosity is twice piqued, in logico-philosophical minds, when the new book turns out to be *Symbolic Logic*. These minds were already cognizant of a Part 1, 1896, of two hundred modest pages. It ran into four editions, as Lewis Carroll called them, in the space of ten months. Despite its austere title it was accessible to children, as it was meant to be. Parts 2 and 3 were already projected at that time, the one Advanced and the other Transcendental. What is now newly before us is Part 2. Modern logic was little beyond its formative stage in Carroll's day, so the more romantic among us might look to his newly revealed Advanced Logic in hopes of finding historically interesting anticipations at least, and perhaps even new light on live topics. The editor of the volume, W. W. Bartley III, evinced and encouraged this romantic attitude in his advance publicity, which appeared in 1972 as an article in the *Scientific American*.

Carroll worked on Part 2 up to his death in 1898. Much

Reprinted from the *Times Literary Supplement*, London, August 26, 1977.

of it was typeset while the work was in progress. Professor Bartley has retrieved the galley proofs, running to 145 pages. He has eked this material out with twenty-eight pages from his own hand, sixteen pages from Carroll's notes and letters, and thirty pages of facsimiles, photographs, and humorous drawings from other sources. Part 2, thus synthesized, is just the second half of the volume that is now before us; for Bartley has also reprinted Part 1 and prefixed forty pages of editorial introduction.

Let us then begin with a retrospective look at Part 1, Elementary. It was not a pioneer work. It was innocent of what may properly be called modern logic, though this had already come abruptly into being seventeen years before, at the hands of Gottlob Frege, in 1879. There was indeed little reason for Carroll to have known of Frege, whose work was long unappreciated; but by Carroll's day Frege's crucial idea had been rediscovered in America by Charles Sanders Peirce (1885) and the science had been progressing apace in three countries. Ernst Schröder was developing it at book length in 1890, 1891, and 1895. Giuseppe Peano had shown glimmerings in 1888 and a firm command in publications of 1893–1895. But Carroll's link with the logical literature bridged all this latter-day turbulence and reached back to John Venn's unregenerate book of the same title, *Symbolic Logic* (1881). Our editor does state that Carroll knew of Peirce, but no influence is evident. Further, he quotes Eric Temple Bell as saying of Carroll that "as a mathematical logician, he was far ahead of his British contemporaries." The word "British" is vital here, but even so the "far" is debatable.

Let me explain the distinctive trait of modern logic. It has often been said that traditional logic treated only of attributes, while modern logic handles also relations. But this contrast is apt to be misunderstood, particularly since Carroll himself emphasizes something he calls relation.

Logic, old or new, traces implications. If one sentence is implied by another, or jointly by several, the connections normally depend on a sharing of terms in varying contexts. Thus, to adapt a syllogism of Carroll's,

> None but the brave deserves the fair,
> Some braggarts are not brave,
> Therefore some braggarts do not deserve the fair.

Now the shared term 'deserves' is relational, certainly. It applies to people in pairs; x deserves y. But our syllogism does not hinge on it, because the term has an unvarying context: 'deserves the fair'. It is rather this latter three-word term as a whole that is relevant to the structure of our syllogism, and it expresses a mere attribute of people taken one at a time: x deserves the fair.

In contrast there is this time-honored example from Jungius:

> Circles are figures,
> Therefore whoever draws a circle draws a figure.

The structure that sustains this implication can be elicited only by attending to the relational term 'draws'. If we bundle this term off as a mere part of two monolithic attributional terms, 'draws a circle' and 'draws a figure', the required structure is lost.

Implications that depend thus essentially on relational terms are what were not covered in any systematic way by the old logic, and are covered smoothly and exhaustively by the new. The trivial example from Jungius gives no hint of the vastness of this coverage. Modern logic is a serious branch of mathematics, and an elegant one.

Syllogisms, for all their slightness, had been the mainstay of formal logic down the centuries. Rules were devised for spotting the valid syllogism—descriptive rules rather than computation. Innovations of an algebraic kind did emerge a few times, by way of expediting the work and widening the coverage. George Boole's work around 1850 was the start of a more continuous development in this vein. At that time Augustus DeMorgan even ventured a little algebra of relations, suited to the Jungius example and the like, but this was rather a foreshadowing of modern logic than the real thing. It was not very systematic, and the coverage was spotty.

W. Stanley Jevons removed some kinks from Boole's methods. Venn continued in this line, and also presented a convenient method of diagrams for testing syllogisms and other simple inferences. All this was again a theory purely of attributes, not relations.

Venn, we saw, was Carroll's point of departure. The departure is inconsiderable. Carroll uses a different style of diagrams, and his algebraic notation adheres less slavishly to arithmetical analogies. His notation has the virtue of distinguishing between connectives of terms and connectives of sentences; this was a departure from the usage of Venn and his predecessors, but already usual in the new logic outside Carroll's orbit. Carroll himself does not strictly observe it in his later work.

Carroll has a compact notation of subscripts. Where 'x' stands for a term, e.g., 'angels', 'x_0' means that there are no x and 'x_1' means that there are some x. Thus 'xy_0' means there are no xy, or in other words that no x are y, and 'xy_1' means that some x are y. To affirm 'x_1' and 'xy_0' jointly he writes 'x_1y_0'. Correspondingly then we would expect 'x_0y_1' to affirm 'x_0' and 'xy_1' jointly, but these are incompatible, so Carroll puts 'x_0y_1' to another use: to mean that x_0 or xy_1. We may guess from this that the algebraic notation is for him less a medium of calculation than a shorthand. The thought is borne out as we read on: he is given to testing implications by descriptive rules rather than by algebraic transformations. In this respect his kinship is even more with the age-old syllogistic tradition than with Boole and his followers.

But he does decidedly improve the old treatments of the syllogism. Alumni of old-fashioned schools will recall that there were twenty-four valid moods of the syllogism, classified into four figures. Carroll reassociates negation with the predicate term, thus reading 'are-not y' as 'are non-y'; further he allows the subject term likewise to be negative; and finally he drops the distinction between subject and predicate. The effect is that twelve of the old moods are absorbed into the other twelve, and twelve new ones emerge that were not traditionally covered. He has doubled the coverage and simplified the rules. Instead of four figures he counts three.

After syllogisms, then what? Carroll's answer: the sorites. A sorites is an implication that has many premises and can be resolved into a chain of syllogisms. Carroll's whimsy has had outlets in his examples of syllogisms, but it is in his soriteses, as he calls them, that he pulls all stops. A typical one has these six premises:

No husband, who is always giving his wife new dresses, can be a cross-grained man.

A methodical husband always comes home for his tea.

No one, who hangs up his hat on a gas jet, can be a man that is kept in proper order by his wife.

A good husband is always giving his wife new dresses.

No husband can fail to be cross-grained, if his wife does not keep him in proper order.

An unmethodical husband always hangs up his hat on the gas jet.

The problem is to find the conclusion, which is that a good husband always comes home for his tea, and to derive it in a chain of valid syllogisms. At this point Carroll does indeed come out with something algorithmic: a routine for symbolizing the premises and successively canceling terms from them. Each such step changes two sentences into an intermediate conclusion, and the process terminates with the conclusion of the lot.

In its opening pages Part 1 is sweepingly ontological. "The Universe contains *Things* . . . Things have *Attributes*." Carroll then adverts to "a Mental Process, in which we imagine that we have put together, in a group, certain Things. Such a group is called a Class." We expect classes to differ from one another only in respect of their members; but no. "Things that weigh a ton and are easily lifted by a baby" constitute one empty class, he holds, while "towns paved with gold" constitute another. Why then talk of classes, over and above attributes?

"A Class, containing only one member, is called an Individual." In thus failing to distinguish unit classes from their members he continues, characteristically, the succession from Boole through Venn. Frege and Peano had by then appreciated how imperative the distinction is, but theirs was another world.

Carroll defends the syllogism against detractors who im-

pute to it the fallacy of "begging the question." This
criticism is familiar and feeble, but Carroll's defense is out-
rageous. He represents the detractors as claiming "that the
whole Conclusion is involved in *one* of the Premisses," and
then he easily counters the criticism by saying that "the
Conclusion is really involved in the *two* Premisses taken together." The children, to whom Part 1 is in part addressed,
are the only readers who are apt to believe that anyone really
claimed "that the whole Conclusion is involved in *one* of
the Premisses." Carroll sets those children a poor example
of intellectual morality.

I have been describing Part 1, which is the reprint. Since
it was meant to be accessible to children, it may be excused
for remaining at essentially the syllogistic level. Let us look
at last to Part 2, Advanced. It is the place for historically
significant bits, if such there be.

It begins with a little period piece on another traditional
issue of roughly the same negligible magnitude as the one
about whether the syllogism is question-begging. This is the
dispute over whether 'All x are y' implies that there are x.
The medieval rules of the syllogism favor this implication.
Modern logic gains symmetry and simplicity by according a
primary role rather to a reading of 'All x are y' that does
not require there to be x. Ordinary usage of these words perhaps varies on the point, and no matter, since anyone can
add a phrase for precision when desired. Carroll comes off
badly here. He professes actually to prove the implication,
arguing from other implications that have no stronger claims
and are palpably equivalent. It is a sorry display of question-
begging, as the editor recognizes.

Carroll is contentious. He presently shows himself so
again, in an impassioned plea for his reinterpretation of 'are-
not y' as 'are non-y'. I casually praised this move, above, for
the simplified treatment of the syllogism that it affords; but
Carroll carps. He lashes out against "The Logicians" for
their "perfectly *morbid* dread of negative Attributes, which
makes them shut their eyes like frightened children"; an
"unreasoning terror." His defensiveness shows itself soon
again, when he proceeds to argue the superiority of his diagrams over Venn's. He objects that one of Venn's compart-

ments cannot be shaded, being the whole of outer space; he knew full well that we easily shade enough of it to get on with.

The rudimentary algebraic notation that he used in his treatment of syllogisms and sorites in Part 1 now undergoes a slight augmentation: a sign for 'or' is added. With its help his three so-called figures of the syllogism are now extended to six. The added forms differ increasingly from syllogisms hitherto so called; but they continue to have three terms, all attributional.

Next the editor interposes some logical charts that he found among Carroll's papers and has contrived, with one exception, to interpret. Most of them are variants of a single chart, best visualized in three dimensions as made up of thirteen points on a tetrahedron. The points stand for 'There are x', 'All x are y', 'No x are y', 'Some x are y', and various more complex combinations, and the formula in the middle of any line is implied by those at the ends.

What next? Back to the sorites! He presents an algorithm that takes the form of a genealogical tree. Given any number of premises, the procedure finds the appropriate conclusion, if any, and establishes it. It is required that each premise and the conclusion have either the form 'All xyz . . . are uvw . . .' or the form 'There are no xyz . . .', with any number of terms negated. (His fifth example exceeds this requirement in two of its twenty-four premises, but he reduces the two to form.)

There follows a series of fanciful examples, some with as many as fifty premises and more terms. Such are the Problem of the School-Boys, the Pork-Chop Problem, Froggy's Problem, and many others. This material is drawn largely from pieces of Carroll's other than the incomplete galley proofs of Part 2. Froggy's Problem had appeared in *Antaeus* with cartoons by Gorey, of *Amphigory;* they are reproduced. Some of the problems Carroll solves by his tree method, with variations. As the editor remarks, an air of sleuthing prevails; "it is almost as if Sherlock Holmes had commissioned Carroll to aid in the education of poor Dr. Watson." Some problems proceed independently of symbolic devices, and these grade off into the ancient paradox "I am lying" and lesser puzzles.

Some of these are presented at length in that leisurely narrative style of Carroll's that we love so well. One of them, "What Achilles said to the Tortoise," appeared first in *Mind* and is familiar to philosophers. Many letters of Carroll's regarding various of the problems are included in the book, mainly letters to John Cook Wilson. The principal controversy arose over Carroll's so-called Barber-Shop Paradox, and spread beyond Carroll and Wilson to Venn, Sidgwick, Russell, and others. It is not the celebrated paradox about shaving. It is a flimsy thing, and can puzzle no one who is clear in his mind about 'if'.

The editor has annotated the volume throughout, often helpfully. In his introduction we find an interesting account of his intermittent quest, over a period of fifteen years, for the unpublished material. He says it all began with uneasiness over the use that Ryle, Stephen Toulmin, and I had made of "What Achilles said to the Tortoise." He wanted to see whether some unpublished papers might illuminate Carroll's intentions. He quotes Ryle and Toulmin as citing Carroll's piece to support their doctrine that universal hypotheses are not truths but mere "inference licenses." He could not quote me to the point, for I have never accepted or written about that doctrine of universal hypotheses. Where I cited Carroll's piece, I was just making Carroll's own point, which is quite clear in his piece, and giving due credit. As for the doctrine regarding universal hypotheses, certainly it was not Carroll's, nor did Ryle and Toulmin suppose it was; they were deliberately pressing forward from Carroll on their own. Still, we can be thankful for Bartley's misunderstanding if it led to this substantial addition to the Carroll corpus.

Considering Bartley's long pursuit of Carroll's papers and his arduous editing, one expects him to be Carroll's champion. He claims somewhat less for Carroll, however, than he did in the 1972 *Scientific American*. He then represented Carroll's tree method as a general method of deciding validity, or implication, throughout the nonrelational part of logic. This, as he remarked, would be an anticipation of something that was achieved after a fashion by Leopold Löwenheim in 1915 and in a practicable way by Heinrich

Behmann in 1922. Actually the scope of Carroll's method is narrower; I indicated it above. Bartley still sees in Carroll's trees "a striking resemblance . . . to a method of 'Semantic Tableaux'" used in recent decades by Evert Beth and Jaakko Hintikka, but in fact this resemblance again is superficial, for the difference in yield is vast. Also Bartley makes too much of Carroll's observations on the liar paradox. But again we can be thankful for some excess of enthusiasm if it was a condition of the service that Bartley has done us.

It is our admiration of Lewis Carroll's other works that lends interest to this one. The volume also offers further gratification on its own account to all who respond to Lewis Carroll's magic touch. Those who are puzzle fanciers, in particular, can revel in the book for many long evenings.

17

Kurt Gödel

Kurt Gödel was born on April 28, 1906, in Brünn, or Brno, Moravia. He was a son of Rudolf Gödel and Marianne, née Handschuh. He entered the University of Vienna in 1924. On February 6, 1930, he received his doctorate in mathematics.

His doctoral dissertation was a proof of the completeness of the first-order predicate calculus. This calculus is the basic department of modern formal logic; there are some who even equate it to logic, in a defensibly narrow sense of the word. Its formulas represent forms of sentences, with variables in place of predicates. Its valid formulas are the ones that go over into true sentences no matter what predicates are put for the variables. What Gödel proved was that every one of the valid formulas admits of formal proof by any of various current proof procedures.

Such completeness was expected. A logician who expected the contrary would have been at pains to strengthen the known proof procedures in hopes of achieving completeness. But an actual proof of completeness was less expected, and a notable accomplishment. It came as a welcome reassurance. Thoralf Skolem in Oslo had already published results in 1929 and earlier which, taken together, may in retrospect be interpreted as anticipating this completeness theorem. Those papers were rather vague on the point, however, and Gödel's work was independent of them.

Reprinted from the *Year Book* for 1978 of the American Philosophical Society.

Gödel had finished this work when 1930 dawned. Before that year was over, his next theorem had been published and its proof had been received for publication; and it was this theorem that sealed his immortality. In contrast to his completeness theorem, this was a theorem of incompletability: the incompletability of elementary number theory. The completeness of the predicate calculus had been, as I said, expected; one merely wanted the proof. On the other hand, the incompletability of elementary number theory came as an upset of firm preconceptions and a crisis in the philosophy of mathematics.

Elementary number theory is the modest part of mathematics that is concerned with the addition and multiplication of whole numbers. Whatever sound and usable rules of proof one may devise, some truths of elementary number theory will remain unprovable; this is the gist of Gödel's theorem. Given any proof procedure, he showed how to construct a sentence purely in the meager notation of elementary number theory that can be proved if and only if it is false. But wait: the sentence cannot be proved and yet be false, if the rules of proof are sound. So it is true but unprovable.

We used to think that mathematical truth consisted in provability. Now we see that this view is untenable for mathematics as a whole, and even for mathematics in any considerable part; for elementary number theory is indeed a modest part, and it already exceeds any acceptable proof procedure.

Specialists will note that in this sketch I resort to vagueness now and again to round off some technical corners.

In the same epoch-making paper Gödel adduced also a further theorem, as corollary to the main one. The gist of it is that a mathematical theory cannot ordinarily be proved to be free of internal contradiction except by resorting to another theory that rests on stronger assumptions, and hence is less reliable, than the theory whose consistency is being proved. Like the incompletability theorem, this corollary has a melancholy ring. Still it has been found to be of positive utility when we are concerned to prove that one theory is stronger than another: we can do so by proving in the one theory that the other is consistent.

The techniques that went into Gödel's proof of incompletability have had utility elsewhere too. They have been instrumental in the rapid development of a vigorous new branch of mathematics, known in part as hierarchy theory and in part as recursive number theory, or recursion theory. The latter has played a major role in the theory of computers.

In the years 1932–1935 Gödel communicated further technical results regarding logical provability in the course of ten short papers. He continued at Vienna as Privatdozent until 1938, but visited America in 1934 to lecture at the Institute of Advanced Study. In 1938 he married Adele Porkert, of Vienna, and moved with her to Princeton as a permanent member of the Institute for Advanced Study. They had no children. Gödel became an American citizen in 1948 and was promoted in 1953 to a professorship at the Institute, where he remained until his death on January 14, 1978.

Gödel's third great discovery was announced in an abstract in 1938 and expounded in full in 1940: the consistency of the continuum hypothesis and of the axiom of choice.

The axiom of choice runs as follows. Suppose a great lot of sets, all mutually exclusive and none of them empty; then there will also be a set containing exactly one member from each. This axiom rings true, and it can be proved as long as the sets in question are finite in number. But for infinite cases no proof is known: none from more obvious beginnings. Yet there are many interesting theorems about infinite sets and infinite numbers that depend for their proofs on the axiom of choice. Accordingly, Gödel's new theorem was welcome; for he proved that the axiom of choice could be added to the usual axioms of set theory without engendering contradiction.

The continuum hypothesis says in effect, of any infinite lot of objects, that either they can be exhausted by assigning each to a distinct whole number or else the real numbers can be exhausted by assigning each real number to a distinct one of those objects. This, unlike the axiom of choice, can scarcely be said to ring true; it rings no bell. There is also a generalized continuum hypothesis, yet farther out. Suffice it to say that these hypotheses resist both proof and disproof from more obvious beginnings, and that they cut a conspicuous figure in the theory of infinite numbers. Gödel's new theorem established that the continuum hypothesis, simple or generalized, can be added to the usual axioms without engendering contradiction.

His way of proving all this, concerning both the axiom of choice and the continuum hypothesis, was every bit as valuable as what he proved. His proof revealed a skeletal structure, economical as can be, that meets all the demands of the usual set theory. This structure, and the assurance of its adequacy, have figured fruitfully in subsequent research also apart from questions of consistency of the axiom of choice and the continuum hypothesis.

What Gödel proved about the axiom of choice and the continuum hypothesis was, we saw, that they can be added to the usual axioms of set theory without engendering contradiction. Now Paul J. Cohen has since proved further that they can be denied without engendering contradiction. They thus hang in midair, undetermined by accepted mathematical principles. We have here a notable postscript to Gödel's already devastating incompleteness theorem. That theorem told us that any given proof procedure, if sound, will leave some mathematical questions (indeed infinitely many) undecidable. And now in the axiom of choice and the continuum hypothesis we have two dramatic examples: two long-studied mathematical questions that are in principle undecidable on the basis of recognized mathematical principles.

Do these results cast doubt on the objectivity of mathematical truth? Or do they reveal unsuspected limits to the power of the mind? Gödel was reluctant to accept either conclusion. His brief subsequent writings reflect a preoccupation with this issue. He believed in the reality of the abstract objects of mathematics and in the capacity of the human mind to apprehend them intuitively. He thought it possible for the mind to transcend formal proof procedures and thus not be bound by his incompleteness theorem. He thought that finer future intuitions about sets might still settle the question of the axiom of choice and the continuum hypothesis.

He propounded no systematic philosophy, but we see him leaning to idealism or even to an old-fashioned rationalism. He particularly admired the rationalist Leibnitz, who had himself anticipated something of mathematical logic. And in a brief contribution to the Einstein volume in Schilpp's Library of Living Philosophers we find Gödel arguing that the general theory of relativity lends support to an idealist position.

Gödel was a slight, frail man. He complained of chronic stomach trouble and was sensitive to cold weather. He could be seen on a warm day trudging along a Princeton street in an overcoat. He said that he and his wife once tried the New Jersey shore for a summer vacation, but found it too cold for comfort.

He had a strong sense of duty. He would pore interminably over the writings of candidates for the Institute for Advanced Study, even though they were only candidates for a year's membership and the writings were remote from his field. He was kind but not outgoing; his interlocutor had to retain the initiative. Such were his achievements, however, that interlocutors with the requisite initiative were by no means wanting.

In 1951 Gödel and John von Neumann shared the Einstein Award and Gödel received an honorary degree at Yale. Harvard followed suit the next year, and Amherst and Rockefeller in later years. Gödel became a member of the American Philosophical Society in 1961. He was a member also of the National Academy of Sciences and the American Academy of Arts and Sciences and a foreign member of the Royal Society, the British Academy, and the Institut de France.

18

Success and Limits of Mathematization

The two conspicuous traits of mathematics are, first, precision, and, second, the availability of algorithms and rigorous proofs. We regiment a technical language with a view to achieving the most efficient formulation we can of the regularities that hold good of the subject matter; and in some cases this effort produces an algorithm, rendering the laws recognizable by computation. In other cases one settles for a proof procedure, consisting perhaps of a compact codification of so-called axioms and some rules for generating further laws from them.

Mathematical language is the far extreme of this sort of progress. Mathematization is what this progress may be called, if only in its farther reaches.

There has been a perverse tendency to think of mathematics primarily as abstract or uninterpreted and only secondarily as interpreted or applied, and then to philosophize about application. This was the attitude of Russell at the turn of the century, when he wrote that in pure mathematics "we never know what we are talking about, nor whether what we are saying is true."[1] He expressed the same attitude less

---

This piece, plus two initial pages here omitted, was my contribution to a symposium under this title at the sixteenth International Congress of Philosophy, Düsseldorf, 1978.

1. *Mysticism and Logic*, p. 75. The passage dates from 1901.

wittily thus: "Pure mathematics is the class of all propositions of the form '*p* implies *q*', where *p* and *q* are propositions containing one or more variables, the same in the two propositions, and neither '*p*' nor '*q*' contains any constants except logical constants."[2] On this view all that is left to the mathematician, for him to be right or wrong about, is whether various of his uninterpreted sentence schemata follow logically from his uninterpreted axiom schemata. All that is left to him is elementary logic, the first-order predicate calculus.

This disinterpretation of mathematics was a response to non-Euclidean geometry. Geometries came to be seen as a family of uninterpreted systems. The first geometry to be studied was indeed abstracted from the technology of architecture and surveying in ancient Egypt, but it is to be reckoned as pure mathematics only after disinterpretation; such was the new view. From geometry the view spread to mathematics generally.

What then of elementary arithmetic? Pure number, pure addition, and the rest would be viewed as uninterpreted; and their application, then, say to apples, would consist perhaps in interpreting the numbers five and twelve as piles of apples, and addition as piling them together.

I find this attitude perverse. The words 'five' and 'twelve' are at no point uninterpreted; they are as integral to our interpreted language as the word 'apple' itself. They name two intangible objects, numbers, which are *sizes of* sets of apples and the like. The 'plus' of addition is likewise interpreted from start to finish, but it has nothing to do with piling things together. Five plus twelve is how many apples there are in two separate piles of five and twelve, without their being piled together.

The expressions 'five', 'twelve', and 'five plus twelve' differ from 'apple' in not denoting bodies, but this is no cause for disinterpretation; the same can be said of such unmathematical terms as 'nation' or 'species'. Ordinary interpreted scientific discourse is as irredeemably committed to abstract objects—to nations, species, numbers, functions, sets—as it

2. *Principles of Mathematics*, p. 3.

is to apples and other bodies. All these things figure as values of the variables in our overall system of the world. The numbers and functions contribute just as genuinely to physical theory as do hypothetical particles.

Arithmetic is a paragon, certainly, of the mathematical virtues. Its terms are precise and they lend themselves to admirable algorithms. But these virtues were achieved through the progressive sharpening and regimenting of terms and idioms while they remained embedded in the regular interpreted language. Arithmetic is related to unregimented language in the same way as is the logic of truth functions; there is no call for disinterpretation followed by application. The case of set theory, again, is similar; it comes of a sharpening and regimenting of ordinary talk of properties or classes. Arithmetic, logic, and set theory are purely mathematical, but their purity has nothing to do with disinterpretation; all it means is that the arithmetical, logical, and set-theoretic techniques are formulated without recourse to locutions from outside the arithmetical or logical or set-theoretic part of our general vocabulary. Purity is not uninterpretedness.

A progressive sharpening and regimenting of ordinary idioms: this is what led to arithmetic, symbolic logic, and set theory, and this is mathematization. Once it has been achieved by arduous evolution in one domain, it may sometimes be achieved swiftly in another domain by analogy; for the mathematical notation that was developed in one domain may, by *re*interpretation, be put to use in another. A simple example is the reinterpretation of truth functions as electric circuits. An even simpler example is the use of graphs in economics and elsewhere. Geometry, to begin with, is a sharpening and regimenting of existing idioms regarding physical space, the space of taut strings and light rays and trajectories; by reinterpretation, afterward, what had originally designated a curve in physical space might be reinterpreted as expressing a relation between supply and demand, or between employment and national product, or between the sine of an angle and the size of the angle. These analogical reinterpretations have fostered the unfortunate conception of mathematics as basically uninterpreted.

Analogy also takes another line. After some subject matter has been well mathematized and has come to enjoy a smooth algorithm, the mathematician may construct another and this time genuinely uninterpreted system in *partial* analogy. He may do so by denying one of the component laws, or by generalizing on some special feature. Such was the origin of the non-Euclidean geometries and *n*-dimensional geometry. Systematic variation of this sort, on a wholesale basis, is the business of abstract algebra. Some of the systems thus produced find useful interpretations afterward, but the driving force is not that; it is intellectual curiosity regarding the structures themselves. There is thus no denying the magnitude of the role played in modern mathematics by uninterpreted systems. It is the tail that has come to wag the dog. What I was deploring, however, in deploring the all too popular view represented by the early Russell, was the failure to recognize the existence—let alone the philosophical importance—of the little old dog itself.

In a higher sense, even abstract algebra and the abstract geometrical studies may be said to be fully interpreted studies after all; they are chapters of set theory. A group, for instance, is simply a function of a certain sort. It is any associative two-place function having a unique identity element and for each element an inverse. But a two-place function is a set of triples, and thus group theory is the part of set theory that explores the properties common to functions that meet these conditions. Other abstract algebras can be identified with other set-theoretic structures in a similar spirit.

Mathematics can stand aloof from application to natural science also without being uninterpreted. Higher set theory is a striking case of this. I already urged that set theory, arithmetic, and symbolic logic are all of them products of the straightforward mathematization of ordinary interpreted discourse—mathematization *in situ*. Set-theoretic laws come of regimenting the ways of reasoning about classes or properties, ways of reasoning that already prevailed more or less tacitly in natural science and ordinary discourse. More particularly, as it happens, this regimentation has been a matter of clearing away implicit contradic-

tions. Once the laws are formulated, however, along as simple
and general lines as we can manage, we find that they are
rich also in implications that outrun any past or contem-
plated uses, implications regarding infinite sets and trans-
finite numbers. Bifurcations emerge, moreover, over the
axiom of choice or the continuum hypothesis or the existence
of inaccessible numbers, where there is a free option between alternative principles without there being any effect
on applications in natural science. Mathematicians are driven
to pursue these matters by the same disinterested intellectual
curiosity that impels them into abstract algebras and odd
geometries; yet in this case, unlike those, there has been
no departure from interpreted theory.

The branch of mathematics that is most widely and conspicuously used is elementary arithmetic. Next come the
parts of mathematics that are built on arithmetic: the algebra of real and complex numbers, the theory of functions,
the differential and integral calculus. The ubiquitous use of
elementary arithmetic was to be expected, since all sorts
of things can be counted and many of them are worth counting. After counting comes measurement. A great invention,
measurement; it enables us to compare amounts of valuable
stuff that does not lend itself directly to counting. It is measurement that makes for the widespread use of the quantitative branches of mathematics beyond elementary arithmetic.

But if the need to compare amounts of valuable stuff was
what fostered the invention of measurement, that use of
measurement has subsequently been dwarfed by other uses.
Measurement is central to natural science because of the predictive power of concomitant variation. Let us therefore turn
our attention briefly to prediction, and induction.

Induction, primitively, was a mere matter of expecting
that events that are similar by our lights will have sequels
that are similar to one another. The larger the class of
mutually similar antecedent events may be, all of which have
had mutually similar sequels, the stronger is the presumption of a similar sequel the next time around. But the presumption is increased overwhelmingly if variations among
the antecedent events can be correlated with variations in
the sequels. For this purpose measurement is brought to

bear. Measurement is devised for some varying feature of the otherwise similar antecedent events, and also for some varying feature of the otherwise similar sequels, and a constant ratio or some other simple correlation is established between the two variations. Once this is achieved, a causal connection can no longer be doubted.

Hence the advantage, for science, of quantitative terms; and they are eagerly sought for the various branches of science. These terms and the methods of measuring will differ from branch to branch, but the purely numerical part of the apparatus will be the same for all. Hence the very general scientific utility of analysis, or quantitative mathematics.

Because of the power of these methods, and ultimately the predictive power of concomitant variation, sciences clamor to be quantitative; they clamor for something to measure. This is both good and bad. It is very good indeed if the measurable quantity can be found to play a significant role in the subject matter of the science in question. It is bad if in the quest for something to measure the scientist turns his back on the original concerns of his science and is borne away, however smoothly, on a tangent of trivialities. Ills of mathematization, as well as successes, can be laid to the quest for quantitativity.

It is in the quantitative that mathematization exerts its most overwhelming attraction. More exotic branches of mathematics, however, uninterpreted to begin with, are likewise enlisted for application now and again: topology, perhaps, or Hilbert space. In such cases again there is the duality of good and evil to reckon with. A happy mathematization can work wonders, and the hope of such gains is always the ostensible motive of mathematization. But there are other contributing drives, counter-productive ones, of which the individual himself is apt to be unaware. There is methodolatry, or the love of gadgetry: the tendency to take more satisfaction in methods than in the results. Also there is the repose, the respite from hard thought and hairy decisions, that a smooth algorithm can bring. In these ways one may be lured into problems that lend themselves to favorable techniques, though they not be the problems most cen-

tral to one's concerns. The rise of the computer aggravates
this danger.

We can sense these tensions already in the following
humdrum example, which involves no computers and no appreciable mathematics. Amid the vague and amorphous matters confronting the social anthropologist, there are the
clean-cut kinship structures. They loom large in primitive societies, and the anthropologist is glad; for they submit
nicely to elementary symbolic logic, and do not need even
that. Now it is good that there is this firm structure to which
to relate other more important but less tangible factors. I
suspect nevertheless that kinship cuts a disproportionate
figure in anthropology just because of the methodological
solace that it brings.

I have touched on the nature of mathematization, arguing
that in its primary form it develops within a science rather
than being applied from outside. It is continuous with the
growth of precision, and it blossoms at last into algorithms
and proof procedures. The most significant continuing force
for mathematization was measurement, because of the benefits of concomitant variation. Finally I noted the danger of
being seduced, by the glitter of algorithm, into mathematiz-
ing one's subject off the target. But I should say something,
still, about the famous formal limits to mathematization
that are intrinsic to the mathematics itself.

Building on Gödel's work, Alonzo Church and Alan Turing
showed in 1936 that mathematization in the fullest sense is
too much to ask even for so limited a subject as elementary
logic. They proved that there can be no complete algorithm,
no decision procedure, for the first-order predicate calculus.
There is, of course, a complete proof procedure for that
calculus. However, it follows from the Church-Turing theorem that there cannot even be a complete proof procedure for
nonprovability in that calculus. From this it follows further
that there cannot be a complete proof procedure for any
branch of mathematics in which proof procedures can be
modeled. Elementary number theory is already one such
branch; hence Gödel's original incompleteness theorem.

Besides these necessary internal limitations on proof and
algorithm, there is commonly also a voluntary one in the case

of a natural science. Mathematize as he will, and seek algorithms as he will, the empirical scientist is not going to aspire to an algorithm or proof procedure for the whole of his science; he would not want it if he could have it. He will want rather to keep a large class of his sentences open to the contingencies of future observation. It is only thus that his theory can claim empirical import.

19

On the Limits of Decision

Because these congresses occur at intervals of five years, they make for retrospection. I find myself thinking back over a century of logic. A hundred years ago George Boole's algebra of classes was at hand. Like so many inventions, it had been needlessly clumsy when it first appeared; but meanwhile, in 1864, W. S. Jevons had taken the kinks out of it. It was only in that same year, 1864, that DeMorgan published his crude algebra of relations. Then, around a century ago, C. S. Peirce published three papers refining and extending these two algebras—Boole's of classes and DeMorgan's of relations. These papers of Peirce's appeared in 1867 and 1870. Even our conception of truth-function logic in terms of truth tables, which is so clear and obvious as to seem inevitable today, was not yet explicit in the writings of that time. As for the logic of quantification, it remained unknown until 1879, when Frege published his *Begriffsschrift;* and it was around three years later still that Peirce began to become aware of this idea, through independent efforts. And even down to little more than a half century ago we were weak on decision procedures. It was only in 1915 that Löwenheim published a decision procedure for the Boolean algebra of classes, or, what is equivalent, monadic quantification theory. It was a clumsy procedure, and obscure in the presentation—the way, again, with new inventions. And it was less

A shorter version of this paper appeared in the *Akten des XIV. internationalen Kongresses für Philosophie*, vol. 3, 1969.

than a third of a century ago that we were at last forced, by results of Gödel, Turing, and Church, to despair of a decision procedure for the rest of quantification theory.

It is hard now to imagine not seeing truth-function logic as a trivial matter of truth tables, and it is becoming hard even to imagine the decidability of monadic quantification theory as other than obvious. For monadic quantification theory in a modern perspective is essentially just an elaboration of truth-function logic. I want now to spend a few minutes developing this connection.

What makes truth-function logic decidable by truth tables is that the truth value of a truth function can be computed from the truth values of the arguments. But is a formula of quantification theory not a truth function of quantifications? Its truth value can be computed from whatever truth values may be assigned to its component quantifications. Why does this not make quantification theory decidable by truth tables? Why not test a formula of quantification theory for validity by assigning all combinations of truth values to its component quantifications and seeing whether the whole comes out true every time?

The answer obviously is that this criterion of validity is too severe, because the component quantifications are not always independent of one another. A formula of quantification theory might be valid in spite of failing this truth-table test. It might fail the test by turning out false for some assignment of truth values to its component quantifications, but that assignment might be undeserving of notice because incompatible with certain interdependences of the component quantifications.

If, on the other hand, we can put a formula of quantification theory into the form of a truth function of quantifications which are independent of one another, then the truth table will indeed serve as a validity test. And this is just what we can do for monadic formulas of quantification theory. Herbrand showed this in 1930.

The method exploits what Boole called constituent functions; when adapted to quantificational notation they might be called *constituent quantifications*. For a single predicate letter 'F' the constituent quantifications are two in number:

'$(\exists x)Fx$' and '$(\exists x) - Fx$'. For two letters 'F' and 'G' they are four in number '$(\exists x)(Fx \,.\, Gx)$', '$(\exists x)(- Fx \,.\, Gx)$', '$(\exists x)(Fx \,.\, - Gx)$', and '$(\exists x)(- Fx \,.\, - Gx)$'. For n letters, similarly, there are 2^n constituent quantifications. They correspond to the cells or uncut regions of the Venn diagram. Each constituent quantification says of its cell that it is not empty. Now Herbrand showed that by distributing and confining quantifiers and expanding conjunctions in familiar ways we can transform any monadic formula of quantification theory, in n predicate letters, into an explicit truth function of the constituent quantifications in those n predicate letters. These constituent quantifications are mutually independent; consequently the truth-table test of validity can be brought to bear on any monadic formula of quantification theory once we put the formula into such a normal form. We simply construct the formula's *Herbrand truth table,* as I shall call it, which assigns a truth value to the formula for each assignment of truth values to all constituent quantifications appearing in the formula's normal form. If we care to exempt the empty universe, as is usual and convenient, we have merely to ignore the simultaneous assignment of falsity to all 2^n constituent quantifications.

Example:

$$(\exists x)(Fx \,.\, Gx) \supset (x)(Fx \,.\, Hx \,.\supset.\, Gx).$$

Expressing it as a truth function of constituent quantifications, we have:

$$(\exists x)(Fx \,.\, Gx \,.\, Hx) \lor (\exists x)(Fx \,.\, Gx \,.\, - Hx) \,.\supset$$
$$- (\exists x)(Fx \,.\, - Gx \,.\, Hx).$$

It comes out true in five of the eight lines of its Herbrand truth table, namely these:

$(\exists x)(Fx \,.\, Gx \,.\, Hx)$	$(\exists x)(Fx \,.\, Gx \,.\, - Hx)$	$(\exists x)(Fx \,.\, -Gx \,.\, Hx)$
$\bot$	$\bot$	$\top$
$\top$	$\top$	$\bot$
$\bot$	$\top$	$\bot$
$\top$	$\bot$	$\bot$
$\bot$	$\bot$	$\bot$

We have now observed this much kinship between monadic formulas of quantification theory and pure truth functions based on sentence letters: the monadic formula has the constituent quantifications as its mutually independent *truth arguments*, that is, arguments that it is a truth function of, just as the pure truth-functional formula has its sentence letters.

It is also possible, by dividing matters differently, to reveal another kinship. Besides seeing a monadic formula in n letters as one truth function of up to 2^n *constituent* quantifications, we can see it also as corresponding to a set of truth functions, or Boolean functions, of just its n predicate letters. These Boolean functions are the *models,* as I shall call them, of the monadic formula. Diagrammatically speaking, a region of the Venn diagram is a model of a given monadic formula if the formula comes out true when all cells of the region are occupied and all else is empty. For example, the formula '(x) $(Fx \equiv - Gx)$ has three models, '$F\overline{G}$', '$\overline{F}G$', and '$\overline{F}G \lor F\overline{G}$'; also the null region, if we choose to recognize the empty universe. The previous example in three predicate letters has 160 models. Clearly any monadic formula is determined uniquely, to within equivalence, by a list of its models. A valid formula is one whose models comprise all 2^{2^n} Boolean functions of its n predicate letters (minus one for the empty universe).

There is a simple mechanical method for eliciting all the models of a monadic formula. It is cumbersome in practice but worth noting in theory. It proceeds from what I shall call the *exhaustive* Herbrand truth table. The ordinary Herbrand truth table assigns truth values to the constituent quantifications that occur in the formula. The exhaustive one, on the other hand, assigns truth values to all 2^n constituent quantifications in the n predicate letters, whether the quantifications occur in the formula or not. Where n is 2, the table runs to four columns and fifteen rows (if we deduct one for the empty universe); where n is 3 it runs to eight columns and 255 rows. Now the models of a monadic formula can be formed from the *favorable* rows of the exhaustive Herbrand truth table, that is, the rows in which the formula comes out true. At each favorable row we simply form the alternation of the constituent quantifications that are marked true in that row, and then delete the quantifiers and bound variables; what remains is a model.

Example: '$(x) (Fx \equiv - Gx)$', expressed as a truth function of constituent quantifications, becomes:

$$- (\exists x) (Fx . Gx) . - (\exists x) (-Fx . - Gx).$$

One of the favorable rows of its exhaustive Herbrand truth table is:

$(\exists x) (Fx . Gx)$	$(\exists x) (- Fx . Gx)$	$(\exists x) (Fx . - Gx)$	$(\exists x) (- Fx . - G$
$\bot$	$\top$	$\top$	$\bot$

The corresponding model is '$\overline{F}G \lor F\overline{G}$'.

So the relation of truth functions to monadic formulas can be seen in two ways: the monadic formula is a truth function of up to 2^n constituent quantifications, and also it is determined by a set of up to $2^{2^n} - 1$ Boolean functions of its n predicate letters.

However viewed, the relation invites extrapolation. Truth-functional formulas are to monadic formulas as monadic formulas are to what dyadic ones? Let us try extrapolating. The truth arguments of the n-letter truth-functional formulas are just the n letters. The truth arguments of the n-letter monadic formulas are the 2^n constituent quantifications. Now the new formulas will be certain n-letter dyadic formulas, having 2^{2^n} truth arguments which are built from the 2^n constituent quantifications as constituent quantifications were built from the n predicate letters. Each of these 2^{2^n} new truth arguments will be, in short, an n-letter super-constituent quantification, and will have this form:

$$(\exists x) [\pm (\exists y) (\pm F_1xy . \pm F_2xy . \ldots \pm F_nxy).$$
$$\pm (\exists y) (\pm F_1xy . \pm F_2xy . \ldots \pm F_nxy) \ldots$$
$$\pm (\exists y) (\pm F_1xy . \pm F_2xy . \ldots \pm F_nxy)]$$

where each '$\pm$' may represent affirmation or negation. The new sort of dyadic formulas to which we are extrapolating will be the truth functions of such super-constituent quantifications.

The n-letter monadic formulas, though they were truth functions of the 2^n constituent quantifications in those letters, were of course not ordinarily written explicitly as truth functions of these. To rewrite them thus was to put them in a certain normal form. Now the same is to be true of our new n-letter dyadic formulas; we may take this new lot as broadly as we please, so long as all are convertible into a normal form which represents them explicitly as truth functions of the super-constituent quantifications in those letters. A natural class of dyadic formulas meeting this requirement is the class of what I shall call the *homogeneous dyadic* formulas, defined as follows: a homogeneous dyadic formula is any formula of quantification theory in which each occurrence of each predicate letter is followed by the specific pair of letters 'xy' in that order, and each of the (possibly numerous) quantifiers containing the letter 'y' stands in the scope of one of the quantifiers containing 'x'. By the same moves by which Herbrand was able to transform any monadic schema into an explicit truth function of constituent quantifications, namely, by distributing and confining quantifiers and expanding conjunctions, we are able also to transform any homogeneous dyadic formula in n predicate letters into an explicit truth function of the super-constituent quantifications in those n letters.

Consider now the nature of a super-constituent quantification, as displayed above. If at first we think of the x as fixed, in that formula, then each line of the formula affirms the non-emptiness or emptiness of a constituent function, or cell of the Venn diagram; and all these 2^n lines together then give the whole story regarding all 2^n cells of some one Venn diagram. Each way of settling all the affirmation-negation signs determines one fully marked Venn diagram for the n predicates. For each particular way of settling all the affirmation-negation signs, therefore, what the whole super-constituent quantification tells us is that that particular Venn diagram is fulfilled by the classes obtained by projecting the relations $F_1, F_2, \ldots, F_n$ on some one object x.

The 2^{2^n} super-constituent quantifications are mutually independent, since a different object x can serve each time.

There is, therefore, a decision procedure for a homogeneous dyadic formula: just put it into normal form and build a whacking truth table on these 2^{2^n} truth arguments. Incidentally we can again exempt the empty universe if we please by ignoring appropriate rows.

We saw how an n-letter monadic formula, besides being a truth function of constituent quantifications, corresponds to a set of Boolean functions of the n letters themselves. Now an n-letter homogeneous dyadic formula can be seen to correspond similarly to a set of monadic formulas in those n letters, and hence to a set of sets of Boolean functions of those n letters.

Another step of extrapolation leads from the homogeneous dyadic formulas to homogeneous triadic formulas, which again are decidable. Their truth arguments are super-super-constituent quantifications. And so on up. In general, the homogeneous k-adic formulas are k-adic formulas of quantification theory meeting restrictions like those noted in the dyadic case; namely, the variables must stand in a fixed order after the predicate letters, and the quantifiers must be nested always in that order.

Our natural tendency to associate monadic quantification theory with general quantification theory is in a way misleading. The monadic has stronger affiliations with truth-function logic than with general quantification theory. All these homogeneous polyadic formulas likewise are, is essential respects, of a piece still with truth-function logic.

What makes the difference between all this and the undecidable general quantification theory is not, we see, the presence of polyadic predicates. What evidently gives general quantification theory its escape velocity is the chance to switch or fuse the variable attached to a predicate letter, so as to play '*Fyx*' or '*Fxx*' against '*Fxy*'.

The mercurial quality of general quantification theory can subsist, we know, in seemingly modest fragments of general quantification theory. The general theory of a single symmetrical dyadic predicate is undecidable.[1] So is the general theory of dyadic formulas in which there is no quantifier

1. Church and Quine.

beyond a single initial cluster '$(\exists x) (y) (\exists z)$'.[2] Perhaps the time will come when what makes for undecidability in quantification theory will seem as obvious as the decidability of the monadic case. That time is not yet.

2. Kahr, Moore, and Wang.

20

Predicates, Terms, and Classes

Let me begin by distinguishing three kinds of expressions and noting ways in which they have been confused. Later I shall make some moves that tend rather to merge them again, though without confusion.

The three kinds are *predicates, general terms,* and *class names*. The predicate may be pictured as a sentence with gaps left in it where a singular term could be inserted to complete the sentence. This is what C. S. Peirce called a *rheme*. I am thinking at first only of one-place predicates, but the gaps may still be many, corresponding to recurrences of some one singular term. Or, with Frege, we may regard the predicate not as composed of signs at all, but rather as a *way* of forming a sentence around a singular term. This also was Wittgenstein's conception.

The general term, on the other hand, is a sign or a continuous string of signs. It may be a verb or verb phrase, a noun or noun phrase, an adjective or adjective phrase; these

I read this paper in South Africa in October 1980 and at Boston University in December. Early portions hint somewhat of "Clauses and classes," which I presented to the Société Française de Logique in 1978. That paper was subsequently circulated in the bulletin of the society. The last part of the present paper is adapted, by permission of the American Mathematical Society, from "Predicate functors revisited," which is to appear in the *Journal of Symbolic Logic* copyright © by the Association of Symbolic Logic.

distinctions are immaterial to logic. If we think of a predicate as a sentence with gaps, then a general term is that special sort of predicate where the gap comes at one end. I am still limiting my attention to the monadic.

Finally a class name is not a general term, anyway not until further notice, and not a predicate. It is a singular term, simple or complex, *designating* a single abstract object, a class. The corresponding general term *denotes* any number of objects, each member of the class.

The schematic letter '*F*' in the '*Fx*' of symbolic logic is quite properly called a predicate letter, for '*Fx*' stands for any open sentence in '*x*', however numerous and scattered the occurrences of '*x*' in it may be. On the other hand, the letters '*S*', '*M*', and '*P*', as used in schematizing syllogisms in traditional textbooks, are schematic letters for general terms. The place holders for class names, finally, are genuine bindable variables whose values are classes. They may be general variables such as '*x*' and '*y*', or they may be distinctive ones such as '*α*' and '*β*' in *Principia Mathematica*.

A major part of the traditional exercises in syllogisms consisted in preparing each sentence by recasting it in one of the four categorical forms 'All *S* are *P*', 'No *S* are *P*', 'Some *S* are *P*', and 'Some *S* are not *P*', known as A, E, I, and O: 'A' for 'all', we might say, 'E' for 'exclusion', 'I' for 'intersection', and 'O' for 'overflow'. The job of recasting can be visualized in two stages. First the given sentence had to be paraphrased in such a way as to say explicitly that everything or something satisfying such and such a condition, '*Fx*' let us say, satisfies also or fails to satisfy such and such a further condition, say '*Gx*'. The remaining step consisted in effect in maneuvering the '*Fx*' and '*Gx*' into the forms '*x* is an *S*' and '*x* is a *P*', with nicely segregated general terms in place of '*S*' and '*P*'. This step consisted, thus, in devising general terms coextensive with given predicates. It was the easier step of the two, for there is a uniform grammatical construction to the purpose: the relative clause. We can immediately convert any sentence about an object *a* into the form '*a* is something which' followed by a contorted rendering of the original sentence with pronouns where '*a*' had been.

The relative clause is often and conveniently streamlined

in the 'such that' idiom, which is simpler grammatically: '*a* is an *x* such that *Fx*'. The bound variable prevents ambiguity of cross-reference where clauses are nested. The relative clause, whether in the 'such that' form or the 'which' form, is not a class name but merely a complex general term.

Throughout the history of modern logic there has been a tendency to confuse the general term with the abstract singular. The schematic letters for general terms, in syllogistic logic and elsewhere, were thus commonly viewed as class variables, and the 'such that' clauses were viewed as class names. At the same time there was a laudable reluctance to objectify classes at the elementary level of logic; one saw the wisdom of relegating them to where they were really needed, in ulterior parts of mathematics and elsewhere. In the neo-classical logic, consequently, schematic letters for general terms were avoided, and so was the relative clause, the 'such that' construction. Logicians made do with predicate letters, always with variables or singular constants appended as arguments. Such is the standard schematism of quantification theory or the predicate calculus, and it has regularly been adhered to even in the monadic case, where Boolean algebra can cover the same ground more simply and graphically. It was not appreciated that the letters of Boolean algebra can be received innocently as standing schematically for general terms, and that their Boolean compounds can be seen as standing not for class names but for compound general terms.

Scruples against premature reification of classes or properties were probably what led Frege to stress the *ungesättigt* character of predicates, or what he called functions: they need to be filled in with arguments. I applaud the scruples and I agree about the predicates. What I deplore is his failure to see that general terms can be schematized without reifying classes or properties. This failure was due to the dimness, back then, of the distinction between schematic letters and quantifiable variables. Notice that even his predicate letters creep hesitantly into quantifiers on occasion. He was still feeling his way.

Once we appreciate the ontological innocence of the 'such that' idiom, we can admit it with equanimity to the language of elementary logic. Now what about a compact notation for it? One might think we ought to keep conspicuously clear of the set-theoretic notation '$\{x: Fx\}$', in view of the melancholy history of confusion between general terms and class names. However, I shall now propose quite the contrary: that we write '$\{x: Fx\}$' for our innocent relative clause, and 'ϵ' correspondingly for the innocent copula 'is an' that is the inverse of 'such that', and that we then simply deny that we are referring to classes. I find that this course is suited to a philosophically attractive line on classes.

Here is a myth of genesis of the notion of classes. It need not be true, though it seems fairly plausible. In the beginning there were general terms, including relative clauses, for which I am boldly proposing the notation '$\{x: Fx\}$'. Prodded then by certain analogies, on which I have speculated elsewhere,[1] between general terms and singular terms, people began to let the general terms do double duty as singular terms. Thus they posited a single abstract object for each general terms to designate. They called it a property, but we may slim properties down to classes for the well-known benefits of extensionality.

Quantifying over classes began thus in a confusion of general with singular, but it proved to be a happy accident, enriching science in vastly important ways that I shall not pause over.[2] And then, in the fullness of time, people whom we can name found that not every general term could have its class, on pain of paradox. The relative or 'such that' clauses, written as term abstracts '$\{x: Fx\}$', could continue without restriction in the capacity of general terms, but some of them could not be allowed to double as class names, while the rest of them still could. Where to draw the line is the question what set theory to adopt. Wherever drawn, the distinction is easily expressed:

(1) $(\exists y)\,(y = \{x: Fx\})$

tells us that there is such a class. Mathematics transcends logic at just this point.

1. *Roots of Reference*, pp. 84–88, 97–106.
2. See Essay 1 above, §II.

What we have here is the theory of virtual and real classes as of my *Set Theory and Its Logic,* but seen no longer in terms of virtual classes as simulated classes. The abstracts are seen now as unpretentious relative clauses, some of which may also be class names and some not.

Logic, then, in the narrow sense represented by quantification theory, can make free with the abstraction notation '$\{x : Fx\}$', but with no thought of substituting such an abstract for a variable in instantiating a quantification. Such a move would require a premise of the form (1), which would belong to a higher level of mathematics, namely, set theory.

Recoiling from that higher level, let us see how neat an elementary logic can be based on '$\{x : Fx\}$' in the innocent sense of term abstraction. This will be the only variable-binding operator. In addition I shall assume a copula; not 'ϵ', however, not the singular 'is an', but one of the categorical copulas, as our syllogizing forefathers called them. I shall adopt the universal negative copula, the E of the mediaevals, exclusion. 'S excl P' will mean that the S's exclude the P's; no S are P. We must bear in mind that 'excl' is not a singular verb 'excludes', joining two class names, but a copula, 'no are', or 'exclude'. The plural verb 'exclude' is indeed a copula, from a logical point of view, and is equivalent to 'no are', whereas the singular verb 'excludes' is a dyadic general term predicable of pairs of classes. When the further step is made of positing classes as designata of the general terms, the distinction lapses.

Term abstraction and the categorical copula 'excl' suffice for expressing the truth functions and quantification. We can define as follows.

$$'p \mid q' \quad \text{for} \quad '\{x : p\} \text{ excl } \{x : q\}',$$
$$'- p' \quad \text{for} \quad 'p \mid p',$$
$$'\exists \{x : Fx)' \quad \text{for} \quad '- (\{x : Fx\} \text{ excl } \{x : Fx\})'.$$

As usual, 'p' and 'q' are schematic letters for sentences lacking any free variables relevant to the context. The first definition thus exploits vacuous abstraction and delivers the truth function 'not both', Sheffer's stroke function. The last definition gives existential quantification, '$(\exists x)Fx$'. Everyone knows how to proceed from these acquisitions to the rest of the truth functions and universal quantification. So we see that the needs of the predicate calculus are met by just the relative clause and the exclusion copula, without use of the singular copula 'ϵ', 'is an'. The embedded predicate letters 'F', 'G', and so on, do remain in the schematism, with variables always attached, just as in the standard schematism of the predicate calculus. On the other hand, the schematic *sentence* letters are a mere convenience, here as in the standard predicate calculus; we could always use 'Fx' or 'Gy' or the like instead of 'p'. Our notation thus comprises just term abstraction and exclusion and the usual schematism of predicate letters adjoined to variables. The exclusion copula occurs only between abstracts.

The reason for distinguishing between general terms and other predicates was that the predicate was not always a segregated and continuous string of signs. This meant keeping predicate letters attached to their arguments. With term abstracts at our disposal, however, this contrast has less point; the predicate can always be gathered up into a general term by abstraction. We could begin to think of our predicate letter 'F' as a term letter after all, if it were only a question of monadic predicates. But it is not; not now. The schematism of predicate letters that is called for in this encapsulation of the predicate calculus is the usual full array, including 'Fxy' and the rest.

However, this line of thought opens up an interesting alternative course of development that is oriented utterly to general terms, monadic and polyadic. Turning to this new course, we reassess all predicate letters as term letters. When 'F' was a predicate letter, the combination 'Fx' was merely a composite symbol standing for any open sentence containing 'x'. Now that 'F' stands for a general term, on the other hand, the juxtaposing of 'F' and 'x' must be understood as a logical operation of predication, a binary operation upon a general term and a variable. I would now write it with a copula as '$x \epsilon F$' were it not that I want to preserve uniformity with polyadic cases. 'Fxy' comes to express a ternary operation of predication, operating on a dyadic general term and two variables. Correspondingly for '$Fxyz$' and beyond.

Numerical indices will now be wanted on the term letters to indicate the degree of each, that is, the number of places. This is because the attached variables are destined to disappear, as we shall see, so that we can no longer count them to determine degree.

Also other supplementary devices will be introduced. The benefit they will confer is the full analysis and elimination of the relative clause, or abstract, and its variables. Predication will disappear as well.

What I am leading up to is what I have called predicate-functor logic. I published on it in 1960 and again in 1971.[3] My reason for reopening it now is that the logic of term abstraction and exclusion which we have just been seeing affords easy new access to a predicate-functor version.

The purpose of the relative clause was to integrate what a sentence says about an object. Its instrument is the bound variable, which marks and collects scattered references to the object. In predicate-functor logic this work is accomplished rather by a few fixed functors that operate on general terms to produce new general terms. These functors have the effect of variously permuting or fusing or supplementing the argument places. Four will suffice. There are *major* and *minor inversion*, explained thus:

$$(\operatorname{Inv} F^n)\, x_2 \ldots x_n x_1 \equiv F^n x_1 \ldots x_n,$$
$$(\operatorname{inv} F^n)\, x_2 x_1 x_3 \ldots x_n \equiv F^n x_1 \ldots x_n.$$

There is a functor that I call *padding*:

$$(\operatorname{Pad} F^n)\, x_0 x_1 \ldots x_n \equiv F^n x_1 \ldots x_n.$$

Finally there is *reflection*, the self or reflexive functor:

$$(\operatorname{Ref} F^n)\, x_2 \ldots x_n \equiv F^n x_2 x_2 \ldots x_n.$$

---

3. "Variables explained away," reprinted in *Selected Logic Papers;* "Algebraic logic and predicate functors," reprinted with revisions in the 1976 edition of *Ways of Paradox*. In its elimination of variables the plan is reminiscent of the combinatory logic of Schönfinkel and Curry, but unlike theirs it stays within the bounds of predicate logic.

In iteration these four functors suffice to *homogenize* any two predications—that is, to endow them with matching strings of arguments—and to leave the arguments in any desired order, devoid of repetitions. For example, the heterogeneous predications 'F^5wzwxy' and 'G^4vxyz' are verifiably equivalent to these homogeneous ones:

$$(\text{Pad Ref Inv inv } F^5)\,vwxyz, \qquad (\text{inv Pad } G^4)\,vwxyz,$$

These four functors accomplish the recombinatory work of variables. One further functor suffices for the rest of the burden of the predicate calculus. It is a two-place functor that I call the *divergence* functor. Applied to two $n$adic general terms, it produces a term '$F^n \parallel G^n$' of degree $n - 1$. In particular then '$F^1 \parallel G^1$' is a term of degree 0, that is, a sentence. Its interpretation is to be 'F^1 excl G^1'; 'No F are G'. '$F^2 \parallel G^2$' is to be interpreted as the monadic general term:

$$\{y: \{x: F^2xy\} \text{ excl } \{x: G^2xy\}\}.$$

For example, where 'F^2xy' and 'G^2xy' mean 'x reads y' and 'x understands y', '$(F^2 \parallel G^2)y$' means that y is understood by none who read it. The general term '$F^2 \parallel G^2$' amounts to the words 'understood by no readers thereof'. In general,

$$(2) \qquad (F^n \parallel G^n)\,x^2...x_n \equiv. \{x_1: F^nx_1...x_n\} \text{ excl } \{x_1: G^nx_1...x_n\}$$
$$\equiv (x_1)\,(F^nx_1...x_n \mid G^nx_1...x_n).$$

It can now be quickly shown that these five functors, applied in iteration to term letters, are adequate to the whole of the predicate calculus. Abstraction, bindable variables, and predication all go by the board. Functors and schematic term letters remain.

For, consider our last version of the predicate calculus, in terms of term abstraction and the exclusion copula. Given any closed sentence schema S in that notation, we can translate it into terms of our five functors as follows. Choose any innermost occurrence in S of the exclusion copula; that is, any occurrence that is flanked by abstracts devoid of the copula. It is flanked thus:

$$(3) \qquad \{x: F...\} \text{ excl } \{x: G...\}$$

where the rows of dots stand for rows of variables. Bringing

our four combinatory functors to bear, we homogenize the
'*F*...' and '*G*...', giving the variable '*x*' initial position in
each. Thus (3) goes over into something of this sort:

(4) $\{x: \Gamma xy_1...y_n\}$ excl $\{x: \Delta xy_1...y_n\}$

where 'Γ' and 'Δ' stand for complex general terms built from
'*F*' and '*G*' by the combinatory functors. But (4) reduces by
(2) to the single predication '$(\Gamma \parallel \Delta)\, y_1...y_n$'. The variable '*x*'
and its abstracts have disappeared. Then we proceed simi-
larly with another innermost occurrence of the exclusion
copula. As we continue this procedure, exclusion copulas that
were not innermost become innermost and give way to single
predications; and variables and abstracts continue to disappear. In the end *S* reduces to a single predication, '$\Theta z_1...z_k$'.
But *S* had no free variables; all its variables were bound by
abstracts, and all are now gone. So $k = 0$; we are left with
merely 'Θ', which is some zero-place term schema, some sentence schema, built up of term letters by the four combinatory functors and the divergence functor.

The five functors that have thus proved adequate to the
predicate calculus can in fact be reduced to four. George
Myro showed me in 1971 that the two inversion functors
can be supplanted by a single functor of permutation, explained thus:[4]

$$(\text{Perm } F^n)\, x_1x_3...x_nx_2 \equiv F^n x_1...x_n.$$

4. This can be seen with the help of *Ways of Paradox*, 1976, p. 298.
The 'p' of that page is 'Perm'. The cropping functor there used is
definable as the complement of our present '$F \parallel F$', complement being
definable thus: '-*G*' for 'Pad *G* $\parallel$ Pad *G*'.

21

Responses

Some of my reading elicits responses in rebuttal or further explanation. Some strikes a responsive chord. The ensuing fragments comprise responses of all three sorts.

RESPONDING TO SAUL KRIPKE[1]

A rigid designator is one that "designates the same object in all possible worlds," or, as Kripke presently corrects himself, "in any possible world where the object in question *does* exist." He reassures us regarding his talk of possible worlds: it is not science fiction, but only a vivid way of phrasing our old familiar contrary-to-fact conditionals. Let us recall then that some of us have deemed our contrary-to-fact conditionals themselves wanting in clarity. It is partly in response to this discomfort that the current literature on possible worlds has emerged. It is amusing to imagine that some of us same philosophers may be so bewildered by this further concept that we come to welcome the old familiar contrary-to-fact conditionals as a clarification, and are content at last to acquiesce in them.

The notion of possible world did indeed contribute to the semantics of modal logic, and it behooves us to recognize the nature of its contribution: it led to Kripke's precocious and

1. From a review in the *Journal of Philosophy* 69 (1972) of the Munitz volume. Kripke's essay is "Identity and necessity," pp. 135–164 of that volume.

significant theory of models of modal logic. Models afford consistency proofs; also they have heuristic value; but they do not constitute explication. Models, however clear they be in themselves, may leave us still at a loss for the primary, intended interpretation. When modal logic has been paraphrased in terms of such notions as possible world or rigid designator, where the displaced fog settles is on the question when to identify objects between worlds, or when to treat a designator as rigid, or where to attribute metaphysical necessity.

Kripke makes puzzling use of Bishop Butler.

So, as Bishop Butler said, "everything is what it is and not another thing." Therefore [*sic*], "Heat is the motion of molecules" will be necessary, not contingent.   (p. 160)

I can construe the bishop to my own purposes: everything is what it is, ask not what it may or must be.

Kripke's positive ruling on heat and molecules is followed by less positive reflections on mind-body identity.

The identity theorist, who holds that pain is the brain state . . . has to hold that we are under some illusion in thinking that we can imagine that there could have been pains without brain states . . . So the materialist is up against a very stiff challenge. He has to show that these things we think we can see to be possible are in fact not possible.   (pp. 162–163)

The materialist will sense the stiffness of this challenge only insofar as he believes in metaphysical necessity. I can read Kripke gratefully as abetting my effort to show what a tangled web the modalist weaves.

RESPONDING FURTHER TO KRIPKE[2]

Kripke writes congenially on ontology and referential quantification, stressing that their connection is trivially assured by the very explanation of referential quantification.

2. From a review in the *Journal of Philosophy* 74 (1977) of Evans and McDowell. Kripke's essay is "Is there a problem about substitutional quantification?" pp. 325–419 of that volume.

The solemnity of my terms 'ontological commitment' and 'ontological criterion' has led my readers to suppose that there is more afoot than meets the eye, despite my protests. For all its triviality the connection had desperately needed stressing because of philosophers such as were fictionalized in "On What There Is"[3] and cited from real life by Church.[4] I am grateful for Kripke's deflationary remarks, for they cannot be repeated too often. But then I am let down by the suggestion that he has "considerable doubts and uncertainties" about "Quine's views on ontological commitment" (p. 327) and that we "need a careful examination of the merits and demerits of Quine's and other criteria for 'ontological commitment'" (p. 415). He, like the others, still thinks after all that there is more afoot than meets the eye.

In the course of a homily on morality in philosophy he rightly deplores that "some philosophical writings of an anti-formalist tendency attribute the particular philosophical views of Russell, Quine, or the Vienna Circle—to mention three examples—to 'the formal logicians'" (p. 409). Forty years ago I likewise was deploring the tendency of anti-formalists to attribute the views of the Vienna Circle to "the symbolic logicians." It is sad that the evil persists, but I find wry amusement in becoming included among its objects.

One of Kripke's moral precepts deplores "the tendency to propose technical criteria with the aim of excluding approaches that one dislikes" (p. 410). He notes in illustration that I adopted a criterion of ontological reduction for no other reason than that it "includes well-known cases and excludes undesired cases."[5] I protest that mine was expressly a quest for an objective criterion agreeing with our intuitive sorting of cases. This is a proper and characteristically philosophical sort of quest, so long as one knows and says what one is doing.

3. Reprinted in my *From a Logical Point of View.*

4. "Ontological commitment."

5. He is referring to "Ontological reduction and the world of numbers," reprinted in *Ways of Paradox.*

RESPONDING TO GROVER MAXWELL[6]

One central plank in Maxwell's platform is that our knowledge of the external world consists in a sharing of structure. This is to my mind an important truth, or points toward one. Structure, in the sense of the word that is relevant to this important truth, is what we preserve when we code information.

Send a man into another room and have him come back and report on its contents. He comes back and agitates the air for a while, and in consequence of this agitation we learn about objects in the other room which are very unlike any agitation of the air. Selected traits of objects in that room are coded in traits of this agitation of the air. The manner of the coding, called language, is complicated and far-fetched, but it works; and clearly it is purely structural, at least in the privative sense of depending on no qualitative resemblances between the objects and the agitation. Also the man's internal state, neural or whatever, in which his knowledge of the objects in that room consists, presumably bears none but structural relations to those objects; structural in the privative sense of there being no qualitative resemblances between the objects and the man's internal state, but only some sort of coding, and, of course, causation. And the same applies to our own knowledge of the objects, as gained from the man's testimony.

I do think there is a substantial resemblance between our internal state, whatever it is, which constitutes our hearsay knowledge of the objects in that room, and the man's internal state, which constitutes his eyewitness knowledge of the objects. This I find plausible on broadly naturalistic grounds. Here then I seem even to be in an odd kind of agreement with Maxwell's doctrine of the relative accessibility of other minds. But I must stress a distinction. What I just now conjectured is that between two men's knowledge of the same

6. This response and the next are reprinted from Imre Lakatos and Alan Musgrave, eds., *Problems in the Philosophy of Science* (copyright © 1968, North-Holland Publishing Co., Amsterdam), pp. 161–163, 200f. Maxwell's essay is "Scientific methodology," pp. 148–160 of that volume, and Yourgrau's is "A budget of paradoxes in physics," pp. 178–199.

things there is a more substantial resemblance than between the knowledge and the things. But publicly observable bodies, still, and not other people's knowledge, are what our firmest knowledge is *about*.

Observation terms are the terms upon whose attribution all members of the speech community tend to agree under like stimulation. Observation terms are the consensus-prone terms, and they owe this trait to their having been learned mostly by ostension, or reinforcement in the presence of their objects, rather than by context or definition. What they apply to are publicly observable bodies, mostly, and not subjective entities, because the learning of language is social.

Thus I do not share Maxwell's doctrine that 'the external world . . . is unobservable'. On the contrary, the external world has had, as a theater of observation, few rivals. I disagree, too, when he denies bodies their color because they are collections of submicroscopic particles. Water remains water gallon by gallon, I say, even though its submicroscopic bits are rather oxygen and hydrogen; there is no paradox in this, and there is none in saying that a table top remains smooth and brown, square inch by square inch, even though its submicroscopic bits are discrete, vibrant, and colorless. The qualities of being aqueous and of being smooth and brown are like swarming, or waging war: they are traits only of a congeries. This does not make them unreal or subjective. There is no call for a predicate to hold of each part of the things it holds of. Even a predicate of shape, after all, would fail that test. It is a modern discovery in particular that aqueousness, smoothness, and brownness resemble squareness and swarming on this score; but it is not a contradiction.

Maxwell's trouble, if he has one, is an unquestioning reification of sense data, Humean impressions, free-floating color patches. If you put the color there on a subjective *Vorhang* or curtain, of course you must leave bodies colorless; for, as Maxwell and I agreed, bodies and our knowledge of them are related only structurally and causally and not by a sharing of qualities. Also, if you keep the curtain, you understandably balk at acknowledging observation of bodies. But the curtain itself is a relic of the days when philosophy aspired to a privileged status, nearer and firmer than natural science. This, not behaviorism, is the excessive empiricism that wants exorcising. Neurath pointed the way, representing philosophy and science as in one and the same boat. Problems dissolve, some of them, when we view perception squarely as a causal transaction between external bodies and talking people, with no curtain to screen them.

RESPONDING TO WOLFGANG YOURGRAU

The word 'paradox' is commonly used, in an inclusive sense, for any plausible argument from plausible premises to an implausible conclusion. Paradox in this broad sense can be a casual affair. A little scrutiny may show that a premise was subtly false, or a step subtly fallacious, or that the conclusion was more plausible than we thought; and so the paradox may be resolved without violence to firm beliefs.

Some philosophers have used the word 'paradox' in a narrower sense, reserving it for cases that compel revision of deeply rooted principles. Such is the usage of those who say that Zeno's paradoxes, the barber paradox, the paradox of the condemned man, Skolem's paradox, and Gödel's incompleteness theorem are not genuine paradoxes. But there is already an established word for paradoxes in the narrow sense; viz., 'antinomy'. So the easier line is to accept the common inclusive use of 'paradox' and then distinguish the crisis-engendering species as antinomies.

Russell's paradox is for me a prime example of antinomy. For Yourgrau it is not, I gather; anyway he does not agree that it contravenes principles 'implicit in . . . common sense'. The question on which we differ is whether there being a class for every formulable membership condition is a principle implicit in common sense.

In any event, both the broad quality of paradox and the narrower quality of antinomy are temporal. What premises and what steps of reasoning are persuasive though faulty, and what conclusions are implausible though true, will vary with the sophistication of the individual and the progress of science; and so, therefore, will paradox. Within paradox, again, the special quality of antinomy will in turn depend on whether what is challenged is a firm tenet of the individual at the time. Besides varying with time and person, moreover, the qualities of both paradox and antinomy are matters clearly of degree and not of kind.

Among the antinomies of set theory and semantics there is indeed a family resemblance, namely a certain air of self-application, or circularity. It is shared also by some paradoxes which are not antinomies, notably Gödel's theorem, the barber paradox, and the paradox of the condemned man, and indeed it is present wherever there is a diagonal argument, with or without an air of paradox. It is not easily read into Skolem's paradox, and it bears none at all on Zeno. But it is so characteristic of paradoxes at their most vivid and of antinomies at their most virulent that perhaps self-application, rather than antinomy or paradox as such, is what wants closer scrutiny and deeper understanding.

For we encounter somewhat this same pattern of self-application also at significant points outside the bounds of logic, set theory, and semantics. A case in the philosophy of science is the paradox of Laplace's sage undertaking to falsify his predictions. Much the same problem takes a serious turn in economics, where a predicted state, for example a price in the stock market, is disturbed by the prediction of it. To cope with this predicament was a central motive of the theory of games. In physics we find an analogy in Heisenberg's indeterminacy principle, which turns on the disturbance of the observed object by the observation of it. If we ever find a unified solution of the antinomies of set theory and semantics, along more natural lines than are now known, these analogies will lead us to expect repercussions in other domains.

RESPONDING TO M. J. CRESSWELL[7]

Cresswell puts his metaphysical question thus: What is it that makes one complete physical theory true and another

7. Reprinted from "Replies to the eleven essays," *Southwestern Journal of Philosophy* 11 (1981), where I answer the contributors to Shahan and Swoyer. Cresswell's essay is "Can epistemology be naturalized?" pp. 110–118 of that volume.

false? I can only answer, with unhelpful realism, that it is the nature of the world. Immanent truth, à la Tarski, is the only truth I recognize. But Cresswell adds helpfully that the question has often been posed rather as an epistemological question, viz., how can we know that the one theory is true and the other false? This is really quite another question, and a more nearly serious one.

There is an obstacle still in the verb 'know'. Must it imply certainty, infallibility? Then the answer is that we cannot. But if we ask rather how we are better warranted in believing one theory than another, our question is a substantial one. A full answer would be a full theory of observational evidence and scientific method.

A quick and metaphorical answer, which Cresswell quotes from me, is that the tribunal of experience is the final arbiter. He complains that my "metaphors about the tribunal of experience never get quite the elaboration we feel they need," and I expect he is right. I can only say that I have poured out the full content, such as it is, of that and other brief metaphors of the last pages of "Two Dogmas"[8] into utterest prose. Such was the purpose of large parts of *Word and Object* and *The Roots of Reference;* and note also Essay 2, above. What I called the experiential periphery in "Two Dogmas" takes form in *Word and Object* as the triggering of nerve endings, and what I called statements near the periphery are recognizable in *Word and Object* as the observation sentences. True, there are scarcely the beginnings here of a full theory of evidence and scientific method; much more to that purpose can be gleaned from works by others.

Cresswell compares my view with Russell's logical atomism and rightly finds them incompatible. "He certainly has no sympathy," he writes of me, "with any theory which would make the atomic facts simple facts about our experience, each logically independent of all others." True, but still it is instructive to compare my observation sentences with this doctrine. They are not about experience, but they are fair naturalistic analogues of sentences about experi-

---

8. Reprinted in *From a Logical Point of View.*

ence, in that their use is acquired or can be acquired by direct conditioning to the stimulation of sensory receptors. Moreover, simple observation sentences are in most cases independent of one another. The profound difference between my view and Russell's atomism is rather that the rest of the truths are not compounded somehow of the observation sentences, in my view, or implied by them. Their connection with the observation sentences is more tenuous and complex.

Likening me to Bradley, Cresswell saddles me with a realm of reified experience or appearance set over against an inscrutable reality. My naturalistic view is unlike that. I have forces from real external objects impinging on our nerve endings, and I have us acquiring sentences about real external objects partly through conditioning to those neural excitations and partly through complex relations of sentences to sentences.

Our speculations about the world remain subject to norms and caveats, but these issue from science itself as we acquire it. Thus one of our scientific findings is the very fact, just now noted, that information about the world reaches us only by forces impinging on our nerve endings; and this finding has normative force, cautioning us as it does against claims of telepathy and clairvoyance. The norms can change somewhat as science progresses. For example, we once were more chary of action at a distance than we have been since Sir Isaac Newton.

These last reflections give naturalism itself somewhat the aspect of a coherence theory after all, and I wonder if I am getting at last some glimmering of Cresswell's discomfort. Might another culture, another species, take a radically different line of scientific development, guided by norms that differ sharply from ours but that are justified by their scientific findings as ours are by ours? And might these people predict as successfully and thrive as well as we? Yes, I think that we must admit this as a possibility in principle; that we must admit it even from the point of view of our own science, which is the only point of view I can offer. I should be surprised to see this possibility realized, but I cannot picture a disproof.

RESPONDING TO DAVID ARMSTRONG[9]

My views regarding the reality of universals have been frequently misunderstood and, I like to think, even more frequently understood—increasingly so down the years. Misunderstanding does indeed linger, and even in high places. Armstrong, I fear, is not alone in it. Here then is my further effort, brief but vigorous, to set the record straight.

Armstrong espouses a realism of universals, and he objects to what he calls my ostrich nominalism. Ostrich nominalism is indeed objectionable, and not unknown. I could name names. What Armstrong does not perceive is that I, like him, espouse rather a realism of universals.

I have explained early and late that I see no way of meeting the needs of scientific theory, let alone those of everyday discourse, without admitting universals irreducibly into our ontology. I have adduced elementary examples such as 'Some zoological species are cross-fertile', which Armstrong even cites, and Frege's definition of ancestor; also David Kaplan's 'Some critics admire nobody but one another', an ingenious example whose covert dependence on universals transpires only on reduction to canonical notation.[10] Mathematics, moreover, and applied mathematics at that, is up to its neck in universals; we have to quantify over numbers of all sorts, functions, and much else. I have argued that there is no blinking these ontological assumptions; they are as integral to the physical theory that uses them as are the atoms, the electrons, the sticks, for that matter, and the stones. I have inveighed early and late against the ostrichlike failure to recognize these assumptions, as well as the opposite error—"mirage realism," in Devitt's phrase—of unwarranted imputations of ontological assumptions. Such was the burden of my "Designation and Existence" (1939) and "On What There Is" (1948).[11] An explicit standard was needed of what constitutes assumption of objects, and it was obvious enough: values of variables.

---

9. Reprinted from *Pacific Philosophical Quarterly* 61 (1981), where it bears the title "Soft impeachment disowned."

10. See my *Methods of Logic*, 3d ed., 3d and later printings, pp. 238f.

11. Reprinted in *From a Logical Point of View*.

How far could one push elementary mathematics without thus reifying universals? Goodman and I explored this at one point. The formalist, we remarked, was already involved in universals in treating of expression types (a point Armstrong thinks I may have overlooked). A formalism of tokens afforded considerable mileage, but stopped short of full proof theory. Nominalism, ostriches apart, is evidently inadequate to a modern scientific system of the world.

Where then does Armstrong differ with me, misinterpretations aside? For one thing, he differs in failing to suggest a standard of what constitutes assumption of objects, and he imputes assumption of objects in cases which, by my standard, would not count as such. His want of a standard in this regard has the startling incidental effect of reviving in his pages Bradley's old worry about a regress of relations. All those relations of Bradley's are real, but there is no regress, for we can define each of them, from the outermost inward, without referring to those farther in. This is because the use of a two-place predicate is not itself a reference to the relation, however real, that is the extension of the predicate. Such reference would be the work rather of a corresponding abstract singular term, or of a bound variable.

Armstrong differs with me also in neglecting the problem of individuation of universals. Under the head of universals we think first and foremost of properties, or attributes. I make no distinction here. I dropped the one term for the other long ago because of a traditional usage, which I feared might be confusing, that limited properties to essential attributes. This is no longer a connotation that obtrudes. Very well; how are attributes to be individuated? When are they to be counted identical? I have argued that no adequately intelligible standard presents itself short of mere coextensiveness of instances. I have stressed further that classes are abstract objects on a par with attributes, that they are equally universals, and that they differ none from attributes unless in their enjoyment of this clean individuation. So I have individuated them thus and called them classes.

At this point, according to Armstrong, I have "moved beyond [my] original position to some form of Predicate and/or Class Nominalism." Original position? My explicit acceptance of classes and predicates as objects dates from my earliest pertinent publications. But Predicate and/or Class *Nominalism?* Such a nominalism would be an ostrich nominalism indeed. It goes with weasel words like 'aggregates' and 'collections' and 'mere', said of classes, and with crossing the fingers. In "Identity, Ostension, and Hypostasis" (1950)[12] I stressed the impossibility of construing classes as concrete sums or aggregates, and the point has been stressed before, surely, and since. I am a Predicate and Class Realist, now as of yore; a deep-dyed realist of abstract universals. Extensionalist yes, and for reasons unrelated to nominalism.

RESPONDING TO RICHARD SCHULDENFREI[13]

"Sentences have replaced thoughts," according to Schulenfrei's account of my views, "and dispositions to assent have replaced belief." Does he mean that for me there is no more than this to thought and belief? Reading on, I suspect that he does. Then he misunderstands me.

My position is that the notions of thought and belief are very worthy objects of philosophical and scientific clarification and analysis, and that they are in equal measure very ill suited for use as instruments of philosophical and scientific clarification and analysis. If some one accepts these notions outright for such use, I am at a loss to imagine what he can have deemed more in need of clarification and analysis than the things he has thus accepted. For instruments of philosophical and scientific clarification and analysis I have looked rather in the foreground, finding sentences, as Schuldenfrei says, and dispositions to assent. Sentences are observable, and dispositions to assent are fairly accessible through observable symptoms. Linking observables to observables, these and others, and conjecturing causal connections, we might then seek a partial understanding, basically neurological, of what is loosely called thought or belief.

This I could applaud, but still it is not what I have been

12. Reprinted in *From a Logical Point of View.*

13. Schuldenfrei's paper, "Dualistic physicalism in Quine: a radical critique," is to appear together with this reply in an issue of the Uruguayan quarterly *Sintaxis* devoted to my philosophy.

up to. I have been preoccupied rather with meaning, and meaning of a restricted sort at that: cognitive meaning. Meaning, like thought and belief, is a worthy object of philosophical and scientific clarification and analysis, and like them it is ill-suited for use as an instrument of philosophical and scientific clarification and analysis. On meaning, as on thought and belief, Schuldenfrei seems to have misunderstood me. He has me denying that 'Tom is a bachelor' is synonymous with 'Tom is an unmarried man', 'since they do not meet [my] criterion of identity of meaning." In fact I settle on no criterion, but I do treat those two sentences as paradigmatic of what would have to count as cognitively synonymous by any acceptable standard, and in both *Word and Object* and *The Roots of Reference* I speculate on supporting considerations in terms of verbal behavior.

Schuldenfrei's over-estimation of my rejections on the one hand, and of my pretensions on the other, has caused him to picture me as proffering some pretty bare bones in lieu of a philosophy. He has me equating experience in all its richness with an arid little S-R dialectic of occasion sentences on the one hand, or assents to same, and triggered nerve endings on the other. This is a third instance of the same kind of mistake that I have just now noted twice; I do not thus construe experience. Experience really, like meaning and thought and belief, is a worthy object of philosophical and scientific clarification and analysis, and like all those it is ill-suited for use as an instrument of philosophical clarification and analysis. Therefore I cleave to my arid little S-R dialectic where I can, rather than try to make an analytical tool of the heady luxuriance of experience untamed. In making this ascetic option I am by no means equating the one with the other.

He does not appreciate that in my thought experiments I am using the strategy of isolation, or of divide and conquer, that characterizes theoretical science across the board. A latter-day Galileo, replicating his namesake's experiment, rolls a very hard and almost spherical ball down a very hard and smooth slope in an almost complete vacuum. He excludes interferences so as to isolate one significant factor. It is in this spirit that I begin with occasion sentences, indeed with observation sentences in my special sense; I thus filter out the complexities, complex almost to the point of white noise, that come of the subject's concurrent preoccupations and past experience. It is in the same spirit that I cleave to the method of query and assent, rather than wait for the informant to volunteer unpredictable sentences for inscrutable reasons of his own. It is not a way to encompass thought or even language, but it is a way in. It is a plan for isolating a clearly explicable component of a complex phenomenon. This basic strategy of scientific theory is graphically depicted in Fourier analysis, where an irregular curve is analyzed into a hierarchy of regular curves from which it can be recovered in successive approximations by superposition. To complain of bare bones is like criticizing the physicist for failing to capture the richness of the rain forest.

Even granted my use of the scientists's strategy of isolating components, the components thus isolated are thicker than Schuldenfrei thinks. The episodes of stimulation are not staccato; they are legato, continuous. More, they overlap. Thus in *Word and Object* I allowed for a modulus of stimulation by way of parameter. Nor is the subject passive; on the contrary it was the subject's contributions that made for what I called "interference from within," requiring me in *The Roots of Reference* to settle for less than an operational definition of perceptual similarity. Moreover, the learning of language takes place mostly beyond the simple S-R level, by dint of analogical leaps that make appreciable demands upon the learner's creative imagination. I speculated on this process in a sketchy way in *Word and Object* and more in detail in *The Roots of Reference*.

Schuldenfrei states in an appendix that he wrote his paper without benefit of *The Roots of Reference,* and that this book diverges materially from my previous doctrines. It does not. Stimulus and response play the same part there as in *Word and Object*. Perceptual similarity is what was treated briefly in *Word and Object* under the head of quality space. *The Roots of Reference* enlarges upon the third chapter of *Word and Object* much as *Word and Object* enlarged upon "The Scope and Language of Science" or, indeed the last section of "Two Dogmas of Empiricism."

22

Postscript on Metaphor

Pleasure precedes business. The child at play is practicing for life's responsibilities. Young impalas play at fencing with one another, thrusting and parrying. Art for art's sake was the main avenue, Cyril Smith tells me, to ancient technological breakthroughs. Such also is the way of metaphor: it flourishes in playful prose and high poetic art, but it is vital also at the growing edge of science and philosophy.

The molecular theory of gases emerged as an ingenious metaphor: likening a gas to a vast swarm of absurdly small bodies. So pat was the metaphor that it was declared literally true, thus becoming straightway a dead metaphor; the fancied miniatures of bodies were declared real, and the term 'body' was extended to cover them. In later years the molecules have even been observed through electron microscopy; but I speak of origins.

Or consider light waves. There being no ether, there is no substance for them to be waves of. Talk of light waves is thus best understood as metaphorical, so long as 'wave' is read in the time-honored way. Or we may liberalize 'wave' and kill the metaphor.

Along the philosophical fringes of science we may find reasons to question basic conceptual structures and to grope for ways to refashion them. Old idioms are bound to fail us here,

Reprinted by permission of the University of Chicago Press from an issue of *Critical Inquiry* 5 (1978) comprising the proceedings of a conference on metaphor at the University of Chicago. Copyright © 1978 by the University of Chicago.

and only metaphor can begin to limn the new order. If the venture succeeds, the old metaphor may die and be embalmed in a newly literalistic idiom accommodating the changed perspective.

Religion, or much of it, is evidently involved in metaphor for good. The parables, according to David Tracy's paper, are the "founding language" of Christianity. Exegete succeeds exegete, ever construing metaphor in further metaphor. There are deep mysteries here. There is mystery as to the literal content, if any, that this metaphorical material is meant to convey. And there is then a second-order mystery: why the indirection? If the message is as urgent and important as one supposes, why are we not given it straight in the first place? A partial answer to both questions may lie in the nature of mystical experience: it is without content and so resists literal communication, but one may still try to induce the feeling in others by skillful metaphor.

Besides serving us at the growing edge of science and beyond, metaphor figures even in our first learning of language; or, if not quite metaphor, something akin to it. We hear a word or phrase on some occasion, or by chance we babble a fair approximation ourselves on what happens to be a pat occasion and are applauded for it. On a later occasion, then, one that resembles that first occasion by our lights, we repeat the expression. Resemblance of occasions is what matters, here as in metaphor. We generalize our application of the expression by degrees of subjective resemblance of occasions, until we discover from other people's behavior that we have pushed analogy too far, exceeding the established usage. If the crux of metaphor is creative extension through analogy, then we have forged a metaphor at each succeeding application of that early word or phrase. These primitive metaphors differ from the deliberate and sophisticated ones, however, in that they accrete directly to our growing store of standard usage. They are metaphors stillborn.

It is a mistake, then, to think of linguistic usage as literalistic in its main body and metaphorical in its trimming. Metaphor or something like it governs both the growth of language and our acquisition of it. Cognitive discourse at its most drily literal is largely a refinement rather, characteristic of the neatly worked inner stretches of science. It is an open space in the tropical jungle, created by clearing tropes away.

23

Has Philosophy Lost Contact with People?

What is this thing called philosophy? Professor Adler finds that it has changed profoundly in the past half century. It no longer speaks to the ordinary man or confronts problems of broad human interest. What is *it*? Is there some recognizable thing, philosophy, that has undergone these changes? Or has the mere word 'philosophy' been warped over, applying earlier to one thing and now to another? Clearly Adler is exercised by nothing so superficial as the migratory semantics of a four-syllable word, however resounding. He would say that philosophy is indeed somehow the same subject, despite the deplored changes. To show this he might cite the continuity of its changing history. But continuity is characteristic likewise of the migratory semantics of a tetrasyllable. We may do better at assessing the changing scene if we look rather to actual endeavors and activities old and new, exoteric and esoteric, grave and frivolous, and let the word 'philosophy' fall where it may.

Aristotle was among other things a pioneer physicist and biologist. Plato was among other things a physicist in a way,

This piece was written for *Newsday* by request as a response to a piece by Mortimer Adler. The two were to appear together under the above title. Upon publication, November 18, 1979, what appeared under my name proved to have been rewritten to suit the editor's fancy. This is my uncorrupted text.

if cosmology is a theoretical wing of physics. Descartes and Leibniz were in part physicists. Biology and physics were called philosophy in those days. They were called natural philosophy until the nineteenth century. Plato, Descartes, and Leibniz were also mathematicians, and Locke, Berkeley, Hume, and Kant were in large part psychologists. All these luminaries and others whom we revere as great philosophers were scientists in search of an organized conception of reality. Their search did indeed go beyond the special sciences as we now define them; there were also broader and more basic concepts to untangle and clarify. But the struggle with these concepts and the quest for a system on a grand scale were integral still to the overall scientific enterprise. The more general and speculative reaches of theory are what we look back on nowadays as distinctively philosophical. What is pursued under the name of philosophy today, moreover, has much these same concerns when it is at what I deem its technical best.

Until the nineteenth century, all available scientific knowledge of any consequence could be encompassed by a single first-class mind. This cozy situation ended as science expanded and deepened. Subtle distinctions crowded in and technical jargon proliferated, much of which is genuinely needed. Problems in physics, microbiology, and mathematics divided into subordinate problems any one of which, taken out of context, strikes the layman as either idle or unintelligible; only the specialist sees how it figures in the wider picture. Now philosophy, where it was continuous with science, progressed too. There as elsewhere in science, progress exposed relevant distinctions and connections that had been passed over in former times. There as elsewhere, problems and propositions were analyzed into constituents which, viewed in isolation, must seem uninteresting or worse.

Formal logic completed its renaissance and became a serious science just a hundred years ago at the hands of Gottlob Frege. A striking trait of scientific philosophy in subsequent years has been the use, increasingly, of the powerful new logic. This has made for a deepening of insights and a sharpening of problems and solutions. It has made also for the intrusion of technical terms and symbols which, while serving the investigators well, tended to estrange lay readers.

Another striking trait of scientific philosophy in this period has been an increasing concern with the nature of language. In responsible circles this has not been a retreat from more serious issues. It is an outcome of critical scruples that are traceable centuries back in the classical British empiricists Locke, Berkeley, and Hume, and are clearer in Bentham. It has been appreciated increasingly in the past sixty years that our traditional introspective notions—our notions of meaning, idea, concept, essence, all undisciplined and undefined—afford a hopelessly flabby and unmanageable foundation for a theory of the world. Control is gained by focusing on words, on how they are learned and used, and how they are related to things.

The question of a private language, cited as frivolous by Adler, is a case in point. It becomes philosophically significant when we recognize that a legitimate theory of meaning must be a theory of the use of language, and that language is a social art, socially inculcated. The importance of the matter was stressed by Wittgenstein and earlier by Dewey, but is lost on anyone who encounters the issue out of context.

Granted, much literature produced under the head of linguistic philosophy is philosophically inconsequential. Some pieces are amusing or mildly interesting as language studies, but have been drawn into philosophical journals only by superficial association. Some, more philosophical in purport, are simply incompetent; for quality control is spotty in the burgeoning philosophical press. Philosophy has long suffered, as hard sciences have not, from a wavering consensus on questions of professional competence. Students of the heavens are separable into astronomers and astrologers as readily as are the minor domestic ruminants into sheep and goats, but the separation of philosophers into sages and cranks seems to be more sensitive to frames of reference. This is perhaps as it should be, in view of the unregimented and speculative character of the subject.

Much of what had been recondite in modern physics has been opened up by popularization. I am grateful for this, for I have a taste for physics but cannot take it raw. A good philosopher who is a skillful expositor might do the same with the current technical philosophy. It would take artistry, because not all of what is philosophically important need be of lay interest even when clearly expounded and fitted into place. I think of organic chemistry; I recognize its importance, but I am not curious about it, nor do I see why the layman should care about much of what concerns me in philosophy. If instead of having been called upon to perform in the British television series "Men of Ideas" I had been consulted on its feasibility, I should have expressed doubt.

What I have been discussing under the head of philosophy is what I call scientific philosophy, old and new, for it is the discipline whose latter-day trend Adler criticized. By this vague heading I do not exclude philosophical studies of moral and aesthetic values. Some such studies, of an analytical cast, can be scientific in spirit. They are apt, however, to offer little in the way of inspiration or consolation. The student who majors in philosophy primarily for spiritual comfort is misguided and is probably not a very good student anyway, since intellectual curiosity is not what moves him.

Inspirational and edifying writing is admirable, but the place for it is the novel, the poem, the sermon, or the literary essay. Philosophers in the professional sense have no peculiar fitness for it. Neither have they any peculiar fitness for helping to get society on an even keel, though we should all do what we can. What just might fill these perpetually crying needs is wisdom: *sophia* yes, *philosophia* not necessarily.

24

Paradoxes of Plenty

In the depression of the early thirties a Harvard doctorate brought only even chances of appointment to a college faculty. One of my contemporaries won the degree in philosophy with flying colors and turned at once to train for the civil service, rather than court frustration in the field of his choice. If a man did get a teaching job, his struggles continued. He would prepare nine to fifteen hours of lectures a week, besides grading papers and serving on committees. He would do his professional writing in the evenings and on Sundays and during such weeks of vacation as were not taken up with summer teaching. He would type it himself and buy the eventual reprints out of a meager salary.

If more money were diverted into academic channels, one thought, how Academia might bloom! Talent would be attracted and relieved of burdens, and a renaissance would be assured. Fat chance, in our profit-oriented society, but a man could dream.

The chance proved fatter than one's dreams. War came, and the government launched research programs related to defense. Scientific advisers noted the value, in a long view, of basic research for which no present military use could be claimed. Support was gained under this head for work in pure mathematics for which no military relevance, early or late, could be imagined. Soon there ceased to be lip service to

Reprinted from *Daedalus* 103 (1974).

military ends; the National Science Foundation undertook to support good science simply as such. By sharing the overhead expenses of the university, moreover, the defense contracts and the NSF grants indirectly helped also the departments that were not engaged in the programs. Eventually these departments came in for direct support as well, through the National Endowment for the Humanities. Funds were found also for indigent students, who were thus spared the handicap of having to work their way through college and so were enabled to compete on an equal footing with their rich classmates. Intellectual promise came to be the only requirement for entering college, and intellectual performance the only requirement for graduating. And there was little insistence on these.

Not a few scientists were lured from their frugal old projects by the glitter of grants. It was not avarice, for the money was not for their pockets. It was selfless admiration of the unaccustomed flow of gold. Also it was lust for power. Imaginations were taxed for projects requiring substantial staff, equipment, and computer time. Scientists thus seduced probably gave up inspired projects, in some cases, for contrived ones. Certainly they sacrificed much of their prized research time to their new administrative responsibilities, and much of their scientific writing to the writing of proposals and reports to foundations. Men who in their youth had chosen the austerities of science over the material rewards of a business career were now in business after all, though without those rewards.

Expensive projects became possible. Science is the better for the vast sums that have been poured into it. To deny this would be more than paradoxical; it would be wrong. The paradox is just that such largesse sometimes works adversely.

Universities prospered, and faculty salaries rose a good deal faster than the dollar fell. Teaching loads were lightened with the expanding of faculties. Secretarial aid was provided and reprints were subsidized. Men whose passion for the things of the mind drove them into an academic career were now spared the old penalties. This is good in itself. It has worked also for the progress of science and scholarship, by allowing scientists and scholars more time in which to be creative.

It may be supposed to have worked for the progress of science and scholarship also in another way: by attracting talent. But here we must look out again for paradox. The trouble is that vocation and amenity vary inversely. When academic life is hard, only the dedicated will put up with it. Allay the rigors and you draw men away from other occupations. The academic life, when eased of hardship, has other attractions besides pursuit of truth. It is clean and somewhat prestigious work in pleasant surroundings, and the vacations are long. It is a continuation, even, of one's glorious collegiate youth. Thus it is that the recruitment effected by improved conditions must depress the average level of dedication to science and scholarship. The dedicated are still there, true, undiminished in absolute number; but a sag in the wider average does little for their morale.

Learned journals throve and multiplied. Existing journals thickened, and new ones were subsidized almost as soon as they were said to be needed. Productive scholars had grown more productive, thanks to the lightened teaching load and the provision of secretaries. This accounts for the thickening of existing journals. The new ones, however, are a locus again of paradox. There are other motives for publication besides that of furnishing the profession with needed truths. There is vanity, and there is the widespread notion, sometimes founded, that academic invitations and promotions depend on publication. Certainly, then, new journals were needed: they were needed by authors of articles too poor to be accepted by existing journals. The journals that were thus called into existence met the need to a degree, but they in turn preserved, curiously, certain minimal standards; and so a need was felt for further journals still, to help to accommodate the double rejects. The series invites extrapolation and has had it.

What now of the paradox? Granted the uselessness of the added journals, what harm do they do? Mere waste of money is unparadoxical and beside the point; my paradoxes have to do not with unproductivity but with counter-productivity.

Regrettably, however, the counter-productivity is there. The mass of professional journals is so indigestible and so little worth digesting that the good papers, though more numerous than ever, are increasingly in danger of being overlooked. We cope with the problem partly by ignoring the worst journals and partly by scanning tables of contents for respected names. Since the stratification of the journals from good to bad is imperfect, this procedure will miss an occasional good paper by an unknown author. Even if we can afford the miss, it is rough on the author.

It was in the increased admittance and financial support of students that the new prodigality came its most resounding cropper. Marginal students came on in force, many of them with an eye on the draft, and they soon were as bored with college as they had been with school. In their confusion and restlessness they were easy marks for demagogues, who soon contrived a modest but viable terror. A rather sketchy terror sufficed, in the event, to bring universities to their knees.

This turn of affairs is explained only in part by increased enrollments, and still only in part by a slackening of entrance requirements. There was a third factor, more obscure, and here it is that paradox again intrudes. If in former times a student went through college on highly competitive scholarships, mere pride of achievement would tend to make him prize the college education that he thus achieved. If, again, a student put himself through college on his earnings, he must have been prizing the education for which he was working so hard. And even if a student sailed through on his father's largesse, still he saw himself as privileged and was ready enough to ascribe failures good-humoredly to his own blitheness of spirit. Mass subsidy, on the other hand, soon loses its luster and comes to be looked upon as each man's due, his return for serving society by attending class and learning what society wants him to know.

Good students are perhaps as numerous as ever, in among the bad. But the atmosphere in which they work is the worse for the hostilities and so are the standards of education. The department that I know best has freed its graduate students of the requirement of general examinations, because these were said by student activists to induce anxiety. It has also ceased to require any history of philosophy for the Ph.D. in philosophy.

It's an ill wind that blows no good. The Arab oil embargo spared us thousands of highway fatalities and decelerated the pollution of our air. I shall not venture to say, in a similarly cheerful spirit, that recent curtailments of funds for higher education are apt to hasten the renaissance that prodigality failed to bring. I offer more modest cheer: affluence was in some paradoxical ways counter-productive, and as we mourn its passing we may console ourselves somewhat with that reflection.

25

The Times Atlas

This is a sturdy twelve-pounder and stands a foot and a half high. Between its dedication to the Queen and its terminal list of errata there are, in three numbering systems, a total of 557 sprawling pages. Almost half of these are given over to the maps, and most of the maps are two-page spreads.

Western Europe begins with a double page of Iceland, just Iceland, a full twenty inches from cape to cape, all delicately tinted green and tan for elevations and white for glaciers and surrounded by the blue sea. Other tastefully sea-girt subjects of great two-page spreads are New Guinea, Ireland, northern Scotland. Smaller countries get two-page spreads too; there is one for Belgium, one for Holland, one for Switzerland. On these three the scale soars to nine miles to the inch, and the detail is luxurious.

Even two metropolitan areas come in for double pages: London and Paris, at a mile and two-thirds to the inch. The London map shows a Greater London which, since we last looked, has been officially constituted as such and has superseded the counties of London and Middlesex. Middlesex is no more.

New York is not forgotten. It and lesser cities are given decent coverage on a smaller scale in insets. One of these little insets actually exceeds in scale the London and Paris

This review of *The Times Atlas of the World*, Comprehensive Edition, by the Times of London, is reprinted from the *Washington Post* and the *Chicago Tribune* of May 5, 1968.

maps, by a factor of three; but it is not of New York. It is
a map of the Kremlin. The book is generous to Americans
in the way that matters: in giving fullest treatment to places
less familiar to us than America.

The intensity of coverage is impressive. Western Europe
is not all accorded the scale of Britain, Belgium, Holland,
and Switzerland, but it is in general accorded a scale of
around one to a million. An inch stands for about sixteen
miles. This is still so big a scale that three of the whacking
two-page spreads are needed for France, three for Spain,
three for Italy. Some outlying regions are also accorded this
generous scale, notably Greece, Israel, northern Egypt, Ha-
waii, and the portion of America from Washington to Boston.
To visualize the scale: Washington and Boston are at diag-
onally opposite corners of the two big facing pages at one
to a million.

Regions thus searchingly depicted are shown again more
sweepingly on a scale of one to two and half million. A two-
page spread on this scale just suffices to show all of France
together, or all of Spain. These maps still show more detail
than we find in most atlases. When we move out to eastern
Europe, the Middle East, the Caucasus, northeastern India,
Japan, Canada, and the United States, this scale becomes
the usual medium of fullest treatment. And very adequate
it is; apart from our familiar United States the detail in
these maps is, for most of us, unprecedented.

Par for the rest of the world is a scale of five million. To
visualize the scale: Mexico, corner to corner, just takes a
two-page spread at five million. This still means overwhelmingly detailed representation when applied where it is
applied: throughout Australia, Indonesia, Africa, South
America, China, Central Asia, Siberia. It takes five such
two-page spreads to cover Asiatic Russia. Try this on a
friend: open the book to the vast two-page map of north
central Siberia and put masking tape over the page heading.
Despite the deft draftsmanship and delicate tinting and the
abundance of place names, he may well be lost.

A scale of five million is thus a feast when you get far out.
This book treats the whole inhabited world on those terms,
besides treating so much of it more fully. Everything is re-

capitulated, for perspective, on various smaller scales as well.

As a cake has its frosting, so an atlas has its maps of the polar icecaps. This atlas goes farther and includes maps of the moon. These are in a prefatory section along with climatic and economic maps of the earth and a quantity of material on the earth's core, the stellar universe, and the exploration of space.

In the exuberant detail of this atlas there is no stinting of place names. This is a largesse which, once bestowed, has to be doubled; for the names are indexed. The index, four columns to a page, takes up nearly half the book. If these columns were laid end to end they would reach more than a quarter of a mile; and there are fourteen lines to the inch. This means nearly a quarter of a million lines; and few entries take more than one line.

These hundreds of thousands of locations are specified in the index by map number and by letters and numerals keyed to the margins of the maps. "A valuable addition," we read in the preface, "is that these locations are also given their . . . latitude and longitude, a combination which no other world atlas so far incorporates to such an extent." Now latitude and longitude are not only admirable; they are sufficient. The editors would have done well to follow the time-honored example of *Goode's School Atlas* all the way by omitting the key letters and numerals. They could thus have cleared the margins of the maps and eliminated half a million letters and digits from the index. This space in the index would have been better spent on pronunciations or areas or populations.

The quarter-mile index is implemented by a list of convenient abbreviations such as "Utt. Prad." for "Uttar Pradesh" and "Vdkhr." for 'Vodokhranilishche." What is more impressive, there is a glossary explaining some twenty-three hundred terms from forty-seven languages. This is useful in view of the policy of favoring native designations on the maps.

The packing of information into the maps has been aided also by another device, a detached plastic panel summarizing the map conventions of color, abbreviation, and other symbols.

In a disarming gesture of realism the editors have ruled up a back page with many blanks for errata, and have filled in a few. Here are a few more. Hokkaido is listed in the front matter as an island protectorate of Japan; it is simply a component island of Japan. Barbados is represented on the map (but not in the front matter) as "to U.K."; this ceased to be true in 1966. Nova Granada is rendered in the quarter-mile index (but not on the map) as Novo Granada; this puts it in a column where one would not look it up. There may be a further erratum in the fact that the tint of Antarctica does not seem to match anything on the plastic panel.

Curiosity is fired by a tiny inset of San Salvador or Watling Island, whose scale is indicated in cramped quarters as $1:1\frac{1}{4}$ m. Does this mean one to a thousand and a quarter, or an inch to a mile and a quarter? The plastic panel explains "m." as "metre"; that will not do. Some measurements solved the problem: it is one to a million and a quarter.

Most of these maps are from the five six-pound regional *Times* atlases that came out between 1955 and 1959. Nothing has been lost, yet compactness has been gained, and with it some additional maps and other material, along with updating of plates. The maps are an inexhaustible store of lore and an unflagging delight to the eye. Seen in the light of what you can now get with $45 in the supermarket, the book is a good buy.

26

Mencken's American Language

The American Language as I knew it in my callow days was
the third edition, 1923, revised and enlarged. It ran to five
hundred pages, counting pp. i-x. There have since been a
fourth edition, further revised and enlarged, and two supplementary volumes and some magazine pieces. What is
now before us is an abridgment of all that, and an abridgment not uncalled for. For all its abridgment, the volume exceeds the 1923 enlarged edition by a factor of 2⅓. (To ver-
ify, add xxv and 777 and, all over again, cxxiv in back, and
then compare print and format.)

Along with his abridging, the editor has made corrections
and, in brackets, judicious supplementations. Between author and editor the 1923 mistakes have dwindled.

Thus in 1923 (p. 164) Mencken reported R. G. White (fl.
1868–1881) as deploring the American *presidential* and
favoring *presidental,* "following the example of *incidental,
regimental, monumental, governmental, oriental, experimental,* and so on." Mencken failed to observe that four of
these six are irrelevant, being built not on Latin participles
in -*ens* but on -*mentum.* Also he failed to observe that *presidential,* paralleling *referential,* is impeccable as an adjective
for *presidency.* Now the new abridged volume still mentions

---

that there had been disapproval of *presidential*: it mentions
it six times (as against twice in 1923, which helps explain
why this is 2⅓ times as long as the 1923 edition). But happily
it skips the reasoning.

This may seem to you like sweeping the dirt under the
rug. Similarly for the next case. Take p. 182 of 1923 on *bust*:
"This . . . has come into a dignity that even grammarians
will soon hesitate to question. Who, in America, would dare
to speak of *bursting* a broncho, or of a *trustburster?*" Appreciation that *bust* means *break* would have prevented this
remark. Now in the new abridged volume I still find no
equating of *bust* to *break*. But the remark is gone.

I see it rather as editorial restraint, reluctance to meddle
beyond necessity. My view is encouraged by some passages
containing the technical term *back-formation*. In 1923, p.
190, Mencken misapplied the term to *prof, co-ed, dorm,* and
the like. In this new abridged edition, the mistake persists
(p. 203) and even recurs (p. 213). Yet the editor knows better. In the course of one of his bracketed inserts (p. 205) he
uses the term himself and uses it right.

Many errors are gone. In the 1923 edition *dead* was called
preterite (p. 285), *you* in *How do you do?* was called objective (p. 305), Rainier was called the greatest American peak
south of Alaska (p. 357), the verb *house-clean* was listed
among nouns used as verbs (p. 198), the open *o* sound in
standard *sauce* was misidentified (p. 323), the British
pronunciation *et* for *ate* was taken for distinctive American
(pp. 275, 280, 284), and *rench* was said to be the invariable
American for *rinse* (p. 281). These errors, hence no doubt
also many others, have disappeared.

Cases of mere bad judgment have been eliminated too.
Thus in 1923 Mencken attributed the "raciness" of *Where
are we at?* to "the somewhat absurd text-book prohibition
of terminal prepositions" (p. 187); surely it is due mainly
to the redundancy. He saw the noun *try* as an apocopation of
trial (p. 191); surely it is rather a freshly nominalized verb.
He saw *kindergarden* as of a piece with pardner (p. 325);
surely folk etymology is more to the point. In each case better judgment has now prevailed—not by substitution, just
by deletion of the injudicious passage.

Cases of bad judgment are also preserved. The vernacular *tole* for *told* was lamely explained in the 1923 edition (p. 288) by assimilation of *d* to *l*. "So also, perhaps, in *swole*," Mencken continued, "which is fast displacing *swelled*." It should be evident that standard *told* is (like *sold*) anomalous: it resembles a strong verb in the drastic vowel change from *tell*, but is weak in taking -*d*. The dropping of this -*d* is mere resistance to anomaly. As for *swole*, the fact is that *swell* used to be a strong verb, preterite *swoll*, participle *swollen;* adjectivally this old participle is still going strong; small wonder, then, if there is still a little life in the old preterite. Assimilation indeed. Happily the *swole* tale is missing from the new edition, again by simple curtailment; but the *tole* tale still hangs on (p. 531).

Some strong-verb trouble even emerges since the 1923 edition. Thus in the new edition an Irish pronunciation *ped* of *paid* is cited to illustrate "a tendency . . . toward strong conjugations" (p. 529). It is parallel to standard *said,* and weak. Also in the new edition we read, apropos of a contrary tendency toward weak conjugations, that "even when a compound has as its last member a verb ordinarily strong, it is often weak itself. Thus the preterite of *to joyride* is . . . *joyrided*" (p. 532). This again is no proper illustration; to *joyride* is not a compound of *to ride,* but a compound noun gone verbal, and nouns newly gone verbal always make weak verbs. Here the editor's touch is arrestingly light: he inserts the bracketed remark "and no baseball player ever *flew out* to end the inning; he always *flied* out." This example slyly shows that he has properly in mind the point about nouns gone verbal, and no nonsense about compounds; still he leaves Mencken's remark intact.

Early and late there is a puzzling insensitivity to the orthography of hard and soft *g* and *c*. In 1923 (p. 232) and again in the new abridged edition (pp. 483f), we read: "The superiority of *jail* to *gaol* is manifest by the common mispronunciation of the latter by the Americans who find it in print, making it rhyme with *coal*." What is really glaring about the English *gaol* escapes mention, the soft *g* before *a*. Nor do I find in either edition any notice of the one other example I know: the frequent American pronunciation of *margarine.* Correspondingly, where *skeptic* and *sceptic* were compared (1923, p. 233), the anomaly of hard *c* before *e* went unmentioned. And in the new edition *Passaicite* and *Quebecer* are exhibited (pp. 681f) with obviously no thought of a soft *c*.

The handling of foreign languages is postpossessing. In the new edition Mencken speaks of the *sermo vulgus.* Look who's talking. Read *sermo vulgaris,* or, following Cicero, *vulgi sermo.* Between editions mistakes in foreign words (1923, pp. 256, 338, 358, 364) have been caught, but one would welcome wider perspective. Thus in the new edition (pp. 374f) *Polack* and *Chinaman* are given under Terms of Abuse, and their histories in English are enlarged upon, with never a hint that *Polak* is the Polish for Pole and *Chinaman* is a translation of the Chinese term. Or again take *a* as in *He musta been.* We read: "The OED describes this reducing of the OE *habban* (Ger. *haben*) to *a* as the *ne plus ultra* of the wearing-down tendency among English words" (p. 534). If we are to dwell on the point, French bears notice for its *a* from *habet.*

"Mencken always insisted, with what seems to most linguists an excessive modesty, that he was not a scholar himself"—so writes the editor, to everyone's credit. It is a credit to Mencken to have insisted, a credit to the editor to remark that he did, and a credit to the hearts of most linguists to have protested. As for the book, in attainment and in evident aspiration it is less linguistic treatise than fun book. So be it. *Vive le sport.* And it is less fun book than, if I have found an adequately neutral word, compendium. It is for all its abridgment a big compendium of varied material, varied in entertainment value, varied in degree of inconsequence. Thanks to its thick index it is admirably suited to sporadic reading.

It is not primarily a manifesto, but it savors of that too. *The American Language* early and late casts an image of its author as *vulgi defensor,* champion of the low-faluting. There is an air of indiscriminate forthrightness and no nonsense. It is murky air, and it blankets conflation. Through it darkly we seem to descry two gathered hosts opposed: regular fellows on the left and a mealy-mouthed ruck of schoolmarms, Englishmen, and displaced Latin grammarians on the right.

Now this illusion of a simple contrast is a confusion of five separate contrasts that are pertinent to Mencken's remarks and quotations. One, assuredly, is the contrast between English in the United States and English in the United Kingdom. A second is the contrast between English grammar efficiently described as by Jespersen in expressly devised categories, and English grammar clumsily described in earlier decades in categories inherited from Latin grammarians. A third is the contrast between speech as a basic trait of the human species and writing as a recent derivative cultural quirk. A fourth is the contrast between colloquial and literary style. And a fifth is the contrast between the descriptive and the normative treatment of language.

Mencken quotes E. H. Sturtevant thus. "Whether we think of the history of human speech in general or of the linguistic experience of the individual speaker, spoken language is the primary phenomenon, and writing is only a more or less imperfect reflection of it" (p. 517). In his next sentence Mencken invokes Jespersen, and in the next he quotes H. E. Palmer thus: "[Spoken English is] that variety which is generally used by educated people in the course of ordinary conversation or when writing letters to intimate friends." Now Sturtevant was alluding to the third contrast in my list of five; Palmer was concerned with the fourth, and Jespersen always primarily with the second. Mencken pictured all three linguists joined as in crusade against a common mawkish host.

Whatever it was that Mencken stood for may seem, for all its softness of focus, to have prospered; witness the new permissiveness of the Merriam-Webster dictionary. *"This data* and *like I said* are all right now," the schoolboy protests when his theme is marked down. "The new dictionary says so." That fixes the schoolmarm.

I shall not argue that this is a scene best calculated to have gratified Mencken. But it does suggest that the last in my list of five contrasts is the one that merits most thought: that between descriptive and normative.

Schoolmarmism comes in part from tampering with facts

to accommodate a poor theory. Insofar it is bad. And school-marmism is normative. Scientific linguistics is descriptive, and good. The new permissiveness of the dictionary, a waiving of the normative in favor of the descriptive, is therefore good. So now anything (if it is already going) goes.

Let us sort this out. Scientific linguistics is indeed good. In particular a purely descriptive, nonnormative Merriam-Webster was a good thing to make, if the work was competent and the job had not previously been adequately done, which is as may be. But there is a fallacy in calling the result permissive; if the book is not normative it no more permits than forbids. And it would be a fallacy also to conclude from the virtues of descriptive linguistics and the faults of schoolmarmism that the normative must be bad. This would be a normative conclusion and a false one.

Behind the schoolboy's illusion there is a feeling that nothing in language is wrong save as a rule-book makes it wrong. People fail to reflect that there remain values in language even if all dictionaries go descriptive, and conversely that normative dictionaries and other manuals of good usage when they do exist are purely advisory, like cookbooks. In this capacity they are useful even against bad schoolmarms.

References

Adler, Mortimer. "Has philosophy lost contact with people?" *Newsday*, November 18, 1979, part I, §2, pp. 5, 13.

Armstrong, D. M. "Against 'ostrich' nominalism: reply to Michael Devitt." *Pacific Philosophical Quarterly* 61 (1981), in press.

Austin, J. L. *How to Do Things with Words*. Cambridge, Mass.: Harvard University Press, 1962.

———— "Truth." *Proceedings of the Aristotelian Society* suppl. vol. 24 (1950), 111–128.

Behmann, Heinrich. "Beiträge zur Algebra der Logik." *Mathematische Annalen* 86 (1922), 163–229.

Boër, S. E., and W. G. Lycan. "Knowing who." *Philosophical Studies* 28 (1975), 299–344.

Boole, George. *An Investigation of the Laws of Thought*. London, 1854.

Carnap, Rudolf. *Physikalische Begriffsbildung*. Karlsruhe, 1926.

———— *Der logische Aufbau der Welt*. Berlin, 1928.

———— *The Logical Syntax of Language*. New York and London, 1937.

Carroll, Lewis. *Symbolic Logic*. Edited by W. W. Bartley III. New York: Potter, 1977.

Church, Alonzo, "A note on the Entscheidungsproblem." *Journal of Symbolic Logic* 1 (1936), 40–41, 101–102.

———— "Ontological commitment." *Journal of Philosophy* 55 (1958), 1008–1014.

———— and W. V. Quine. "Some theorems on definability and decidability." *Journal of Symbolic Logic* 17 (1952), 179–187.

Cohen, P. J. *Set Theory and the Continuum Hypothesis*. New York: Benjamin, 1966.

Davidson, Donald. "The logical form of action sentences." In Rescher, pp. 81–95.

———— "On the very idea of a conceptual scheme." *Proceedings and Addresses of the American Philosophical Association* 47 (1974), 5–20.

———— and Jaakko Hintikka, eds. *Words and Objections*. Dordrecht: Reidel, 1969.

De Morgan, Augustus. "On the syllogism, no. iv, and on the logic of relations." *Transactions of the Cambridge Philosophical Society* 10 (1864), 173–230.

Devitt, Michael. " 'Ostrich nominalism' or 'mirage realism'?" *Pacific Philosophical Quarterly* 61 (1981), in press.

Dewey, John. *Experience and Nature*. La Salle, Ill.: Open Court, 1925.

Duhem, Pierre. *La théorie physique: son objet et sa structure*. Paris, 1906.

Dummett, Michael. *Truth and Other Enigmas*. Cambridge, Mass.: Harvard University Press, 1978.

Evans, Gareth, and John McDowell, eds. *Truth and Meaning*. Oxford: Oxford University Press, 1976.

Fann, K. T., ed. *Symposium on J. L. Austin*. London: Routledge, 1969.

Føllesdal, Dagfinn. "Knowledge, identity, and existence." *Theoria* 33 (1967), 1–27.

Frege, Gottlob. *Begriffsschrift*. Halle, 1879.

——— *Funktion und Begriff*. Jena, 1891.

Geach, Peter. *Reference and Generality*. Ithaca: Cornell University Press, 1962.

——— *Logic Matters*, Oxford: Blackwell, 1972.

Gödel, Kurt. *The Consistency of the Continuum Hypothesis*. Princeton: Princeton University Press, 1940.

——— "Die Vollständigkeit der Axiome des logischen Funktionenkalküls." *Monatshefte für Mathematik und Physik* 37 (1930), 349–360.

——— "Ueber formal unentscheidbare Sätze der Principia Mathematica und verwandter Systeme." Ibid., 38 (1931), 173–198.

Goodman, Nelson. *Ways of Worldmaking*. Indianapolis: Hackett, 1978.

——— and W. V. Quine. "Steps toward a constructive nominalism." *Journal of Symbolic Logic* 12 (1947), 97–122.

Hahn, Hans. *Ueberflüssige Wesenheiten*. Vienna, 1930.

Herbrand, Jacques. *Ecrits logiques*. Paris: Presses Universitaires de France, 1968.

Hintikka, Jaakko. *Knowledge and Belief*. Ithaca: Cornell University Press, 1962.

——— *The Intentions of Intentionality and Other New Models for Modality*. Boston: Reidel, 1975.

Humphries, B. M. "Indeterminacy of translation and theory." *Journal of Philosophy* 67 (1970), 167–178.

Jevons, W. S. *Pure Logic*. London, 1864.

Kahr, A. S., E. F. Moore, and Hao Wang. "Entscheidungsproblem reduced to the AEA case." *Proceedings of the National Academy of Sciences* 48 (1962), 365–377.

Kaplan, David. "Quantifying in." In Davidson and Hintikka, pp. 206–242.

Kripke, Saul. "A completeness theorem in modal logic." *Journal of Symbolic Logic* 24 (1959), 1–11.

Löwenheim, Leopold. "Ueber Möglichkeit im Relativkalkül." *Mathematische Annalen* 76 (1915), 447–470.

Macdonald, G. F., ed. *Perception and Identity: Essays Presented to A. J. Ayer.* London: Macmillan, 1979.

Mencken, H. L. *The American Language.* Abridged ed. edited by R. J. McDavid, Jr. New York: Knopf, 1963.

Munitz, M. K., ed. *Identity and Individuation.* New York: New York University Press, 1971.

Nelson, R. J. "On machine expectation." *Synthese* 31 (1975), 129–139.

Ogden, C. K. *Bentham's Theory of Fictions.* London: Routledge, 1932.

Peacocke, Christopher. "An appendix to David Wiggins' 'Note.'" In Evans and McDowell, pp. 313–324.

Peano, Giuseppe. *Formulaire de mathématiques,* vol. 1. Turin, 1895.

Peirce, C. S. *Collected Papers,* vols. 2–4. Cambridge, Mass.: Harvard University Press, 1932–1933.

Quine, W. V. *Mathematical Logic.* New York, 1940. Rev. ed., Cambridge, Mass.: Harvard University Press, 1951.

───── *From a Logical Point of View.* Cambridge, Mass.: Harvard University Press, 1953. 2d ed., 1961.

───── *Word and Object.* Cambridge, Mass.: MIT Press, 1960.

───── *Set Theory and Its Logic.* Cambridge, Mass.: Harvard University Press, 1963. Rev. ed., 1969.

───── *Selected Logic Papers.* New York: Random House, 1966.

───── *The Ways of Paradox and Other Essays.* New York, 1966. Enlarged ed., Cambridge, Mass.: Harvard University Press, 1976.

───── *Ontological Relativity and Other Essays.* New York: Columbia University Press, 1969.

───── *Methods of Logic.* 3d ed. New York: Holt, 1972.

───── *The Roots of Reference.* La Salle, Ill.: Open Court, 1974.

───── "Designation and existence." *Journal of Philosophy* 36 (1939), 701–709.

───── "On empirically equivalent systems of the world." *Erkenntnis* 9 (1975), 313–328.

Ramsey, F. P. *The Foundations of Mathematics.* London: Routledge, 1931.

───── "Theories." In *The Foundations of Mathematics,* pp. 212–236.

Rescher, Nicholas, ed. *The Logic of Action and Preference.* Pittsburgh: Pittsburgh University Press, 1967.

Russell, Bertrand. *The Principles of Mathematics.* Cambridge, Eng., 1903.

───── *The Problems of Philosophy.* New York, 1912.

───── *Our Knowledge of the External World.* New York and London, 1914.

───── *Mysticism and Logic and Other Essays.* London, 1918.

───── *Analysis of Mind.* London, 1921.

───── *Analysis of Matter.* New York, 1927.

───── *Inquiry into Meaning and Truth.* New York: Norton, 1940.

────── *Human Knowledge*. New York: Simon and Schuster, 1948.

────── *Logic and Knowledge*. London: Allen and Unwin, 1956.

────── "Meinong's theory of complexes and assumptions." *Mind* 13 (1904), 204–219, 336–354, 509–524.

────── "On denoting." *Mind* 14 (1905), 479–493. Reprinted in *Logic and Knowledge*.

────── "Mathematical logic as based on the theory of types." *American Journal of Mathematics* 30 (1908), 222–262. Reprinted in *Logic and Knowledge*.

────── "The philosophy of logical atomism." *Monist* 28 (1918), 495–527; 29 (1919), 32–63, 190–222, 345–380. Reprinted in *Logic and Knowledge*.

Ryle, Gilbert. *Dilemmas*. Cambridge, Eng., 1954.

Schilpp, P. A., ed. *The Philosophy of Bertrand Russell*. Evanston, 1944, and New York: Harper, 1963.

────── *Albert Einstein: Philosophy-Scientist*. New York: Tudor, 1951.

────── and L. E. Hahn, eds. *The Philosophy of W. V. Quine*. La Salle, Ill.: Open Court, forthcoming.

Schlick, Moritz. *Fragen der Ethik*. Vienna, 1930.

Schröder, Ernst. *Der Operationskreis des Logikkalkuls*. Leipzig, 1877.

Shahan, R., and C. Swoyer, eds. *Essays on the Philosophy of W. V. Quine*. Norman: University of Oklahoma Press, 1979.

Skolem, Thoralf. "Ueber die mathematische Logik." *Norsk Matematisk Tidsskrift* 10 (1928), 125–142.

Sleigh, R. C. "On a proposed system of epistemic logic." *Noûs* 2 (1968), 391–398.

Smart, J. J. C. *Philosophy and Scientific Realism*. London: Routledge, 1964.

────── "The methods of ethics and the methods of science." *Journal of Philosophy* 62 (1965), 344–349.

Tarski, Alfred. *Logic, Semantics, Metamathematics*. Oxford: Clarendon Press, 1956.

Times Atlas of the World. London, 1968.

Tinbergen, Nikolaas. *The Herring Gull's World*. London: Collins, 1953.

Tooke, John Horne. Ἔπεα πτερόεντα; or, *The Diversions of Purley*, vol. 1. London, 1786. Boston, 1806.

Tracy, David. "Metaphor and religion: the test case of Christian texts." *Critical Inquiry* 5 (1978), 91–106.

Turing, A. M. "On computable numbers." *Proceedings of the London Mathematical Society* 42 (1937), 230–266; 43 (1938), 544f.

Unger, Peter. "I do not exist." In Macdonald, pp. 235–251.

Urmson, J. O. "On Austin's method." In Fann, pp. 76–86.

Venn, John. *Symbolic Logic*. London, 1881, 1894.

Von Neumann, John. "Eine Axiomatisierung der Mengenlehre." *Journal für reine und angewandte Mathematik* 154 (1925), 219–240.

Waismann, Friedrich. "Verifiability." *Proceedings of the Aristotelian Society* suppl. vol. 19 (1945), 119–150.

Whitehead, A. N., and Bertrand Russell. *Principia Mathematica*, vol. 1. Cambridge, Eng., 1910. 2d ed., 1925.

Williams, Bernard. *Morality*. New York: Harper, 1972.

Williams, D. C. *Principles of Empirical Realism*. Springfield, Ill.: Thomas, 1966.

Wittgenstein, Ludwig. *Tractatus Logico-Philosophicus*. New York and London, 1922.

———— *Philosophical Investigations*. Oxford: Blackwell, 1963.

Wright, Crispin. "Language mastery and the sorites paradox." In Evans and McDowell, pp. 223–247.

Index